ONE HOLY
Passion
HOLY

GROWING DEEPER IN YOUR WALK WITH GOD

ONE

HOLY

Passion

COMPILED BY JUDITH COUCHMAN

WATERBROOK
PRESS

COLORADO SPRINGS

ONE HOLY PASSION
PUBLISHED BY WATERBROOK PRESS
5446 North Academy Boulevard, Suite 200
Colorado Springs, Colorado 80918
A division of Bantam Doubleday Dell Publishing Group, Inc.

FOR OPAL STOREY COUCHMAN

a woman who belongs
in this book

Contents

wish I had some great passion in my life," my friend says wistfully as she shifts uneasily in her chair. "Something to do or believe in that really grabs my heart and motivates me to act."
I nod, thinking how ordinary life can be, filling up with mundane and repetitive tasks and, for the most part, handing us what feels like obscurity. My friend expresses a longing buried deep within many women's souls: the desire to be someone, to accomplish something, to make life count. The drive to participate in a grand significance much larger than ourselves.

Yet at the same time, passion scares us. If we're too involved in a mission, will we be consumed, charred into a shell of a person? Will we be so engulfed by someone that the intensity shatters our identity? Will anyone understand the ache, the restlessness, the risk, the determination? After all, we're told to stay sensible, erect boundaries, protect the status quo. We're to keep such loves where they belong: behind closed doors or, better yet, far from us.

This is good advice if we're prone toward derelict loves and destructive behaviors, applying our zeal to the self-centered and sinful. But neither "playing it safe" nor crimes of passion are the way of Christ. "Teacher, which is the greatest commandment in the Law?" a religious leader once asked Jesus. He replied, "Love the Lord your God with all your heart and with all your soul and with all your mind" (Matthew 22:36). The Lord insists that He be our Beloved, the Lover who consumes but does not scorch us, the mission from which we launch our lives without fear of failure. He is the truly safe place to channel our desire, to embrace meaning, to participate in an eternal story grander than our own.

Secure in this relationship—at times nestling in the Lord's arms, at times brandishing His shield of faith—we can unleash our passion. Because He is the trustworthy one, we can surrender all. Take up a cross. Lose our life to find it. Forgive unreasonably. Work faithfully. Love lavishly. Rest peacefully. Be our true but unfettered selves...

But how? How in the midst of people, programs, and pressure do we stoke the fires of spiritual passion? Only by relationship. Bit by bit, day by day, we faithfully (but not flawlessly) nurture our love life with the Lord. We stir the embers within before flaming into the world.

In this book you'll meet women who, though fraught with the urgent and ordinary, have cultivated their desire for the Savior. They whole-heartedly share their stories about loving the Lord, hiding away with Him, feasting on His words, listening for His voice, and enjoying His presence. And from their own struggles and triumphs, they impart wisdom about embracing God's forgiveness, trusting His ways, living by faith, accepting His comfort, and asking for His help.

"But mere talk is useless," writes contributor Lois Mowday Rabey. "Our thoughts, behavior, and involvement have to line up with a passion for Christ—if we want to have a truly passionate life." Accordingly, it's my hope that these pages will not only inspire and encourage you, but also motivate and usher you into an all-encompassing relationship with Him.

May He be your one, holy passion.

—Judith Couchman

Loving the God Who Cares

Divine love is a sacred flower, which in its early bud is

happiness, and in its full bloom is heaven.

— ELEANOR LOUISA HERVEY

THE FACT OF HIS PRESENCE

AMY CARMICHAEL

here was a year a long time ago, before our Indian family as it is now had been created, when I had to be left alone because illness had forced my fellow missionaries to go home on furlough.

That year began in the hour when I stood on the verandah of our three-room bungalow, listening to the scrunch of the wheels of the bullock cart as it turned on the rough gravel and drove unwillingly away. The cry of a child in delirium seemed to fill the house (for a little girl I was nursing was very ill; she almost died that night). There was no one else in the house. The servants had gone to their homes in the village, and the Indian woman who would presently help me had not come yet. The rooms had that forlorn, deserted air that rooms always wear just after their owners have gone.

But I was not lonely. There was something new in the "feel" of the house, familiar and yet new, and that sense of a light in a dim place, and an infinitely loving, brooding Presence near (but "near" is too distant a word) was an abiding strength.

But I know it is not the sense of His presence, it is the *fact* of His presence that is our strength and stay. And yet it is comforting when a mother makes some little sign, or speaks some little word to a child who does not see her. And when our Father deals so tenderly with us, then we are very humbly grateful and we store such memories in our heart. And when there is not any feeling we rest on His bare word, "Lo, I am with you always, all the days, and all day long." And we are content.

The bright flowers of the edelweiss waiting to be gathered among the rough rocks of difficult circumstances—we may call the consolations of God what we will—who are we that we should find such comforts anywhere? Love prepared, Love planted, Love led us to these enchanting discoveries. A child cannot bear to enjoy delight alone; it turns to its nearest friend with a shout of joy and shares its treasures. Turn so to thy Nearest, soul beloved. Speak thy quick thanks and share thy joy. Offer not the discourtesy of remembering thy Unseen Companion only when nettles sting thee, and thorns prick thee, and thy feet are cut on the stones.

Two

THE GREATEST JOY IS HIS LOVE

BARBARA JOHNSON

One of the happiest phrases in all of Scripture is tucked away in 1 John 4:8: "God is love." And I like to add, "God is joy." To know and feel God's love is to know the deep kind of abiding joy that you want to splash all over others.

Jesus reassured us that He would not leave us comfortless (John 14:18). He did not promise endless days of ease, but rather love and growth as we travel over the bumps and washouts in life. He didn't say we would all ride in limos. We might make our trip in a beat-up station wagon, a pickup truck, on a bicycle, or even in a wheelchair. No matter how we travel, the important thing is feeling God's breath upon us. We need a quickening that lets us know God *is* love and we can have fellowship with Him.

Sometimes it helps to get away alone in a lovely setting. It could be at the ocean with the waves crashing on the beach, or it might be while bobbing around in a sailboat or just walking along a path and feeling the breeze blowing through the trees.

But God's love can happen *anywhere*. Once it happened to me at the Department of Motor Vehicles office when I was selecting a personalized license plate for my husband. As I looked through the giant book of license-plate names that had already been used, I realized that my own name is written in another book that is much more important—the Lamb's Book of Life—and that I am forever a daughter of the King. God reminded me that I am His child. I am royalty! God's warm comfort blanket enfolded me with the assurance of His care. I felt His presence so strongly that I had tears in my eyes.

But the specific place really doesn't matter. Being marinated in God's love is what counts. It's your personal relationship with God that makes the difference and brings the joy from His fountain of life.

Three

OUR DETERMINED AND RELENTLESS GOD

JAN JOHNSON

"Describe God," I challenged a group of high-school students.

"He's like Santa Claus...a detached Father Time...Mother Nature...a Cosmic Security Guard watching our every move...the Good Witch of the North from *The Wizard of Oz*," came back to me.

Sadly, even many Christians don't have a clear picture of God's involvement in their lives. Some have reduced Him to a warehouse clerk filling their mail-order prayer requests. Others perceive Him as a fair-weather friend who abandons them when illness or trouble darkens their lives. Even those who view Him as a powerful, caring Creator may under-estimate the strength of His unswerving love.

Our heavenly Father is like the persistent owner of the vineyard in Jesus' parable (Matthew 21:33-41). Nothing deterred him—not the beating and killing of servant after servant, not even the death of his son.

God is the same with us: Despite our response, He never wavers in calling us to Himself.

The servants in this parable represent the Old Testament prophets who warned Israel against idol worship. God used them to run after His people, Israel, persuading them to return to Him. One such prophet, Hosea, demonstrated God's stubborn love for idolatrous Israel. At God's command, Hosea married Gomer as an object lesson. As Israel continued her flagrant adultery, God built a hedge around her so that she could not find her lovers (Hosea 2:6-7). When she refused to acknowledge God as the source of her blessings, He withdrew them (Hosea 2:9-13).

In the same way, God sometimes puts barriers in our paths and withholds blessings to draw our attention back to Him. Although Gomer rejected Hosea, God told him to go after her—just as He seeks after us when we are rebellious. Hosea bought Gomer back, as God bought us with the price of His Son (Hosea 3:1-2).

Hosea's message is clear: God loves us with a persistent, unfailing love. Like the shepherd in the parable of the lost sheep, He will risk everything to find one lost lamb (Luke 15:3-7). A percentage will not do; He wants every person to come to Him.

God does not just prefer or hope that we choose to follow Him. He "wants all men to be saved and to come to a knowledge of the truth" (1 Timothy 2:4). He accomplished His plan of reconciliation through Jesus (Genesis 12:3; Galatians 3:8).

In his poem "The Hound of Heaven," Francis Thompson captured God's quiet determination:

From those strong Feet that followed, followed after,
But with unhurrying chase,

And unperturbed pace,
Deliberate speed, majestic instancy,
They beat—and a Voice beat
More instant than the Feet—
"All things betray thee, who betrayest Me."

God diligently trails after us without hurrying us. He speaks to us, letting us know that apart from Him we will never be complete. He does not just say, "I love you." He constantly shows us how much.

Four

I Can't Make It on My Own, Lord

COLLEEN TOWNSEND EVANS

Poor. I can't imagine anyone *wanting* to be poor, to be totally destitute, in need, anxious, hopeless, frightened. Surely our loving Lord doesn't want this for us?

Yet Jesus says, "Blessed are the poor in spirit: for theirs is the kingdom of heaven" (Matthew 5:3, KJV).

There were many poor people sitting at Jesus' feet when He spoke these words, and He always identified Himself with them. In fact, He told His followers that as they served the "least of these," His brothers and sisters, they would actually be serving Him. But He wasn't telling the poor in the crowd that day that they never had it so good. No, Jesus had great compassion for human need, and the sight of the suffering poor grieved Him. Obviously He was talking about something beyond physical need.

Yes, now there seems to be new meaning in the word *poor*. I think in terms of the poverty we're trying to eliminate from our world: hunger, starvation, disease, ignorance. But there is another kind of poverty—

devastating, if not as visible. There is a poverty of the spirit. And that's what Jesus is talking about in the first beatitude.

"Blessed are the poor in *spirit*." This seems to be the center from which the other beatitudes radiate. For unless we know how poor we are without Christ, we'll never reach out for Him. If we feel we can take care of ourselves, why ask for help—even from God?

Come to think of it, the most joyous people I know are those who have tried and failed—even hit bottom—and then reached out for help. Realizing their spiritual bankruptcy, they asked Jesus to take over their lives. They entered the kingdom through the door of their own need, and they were met by God's grace.

They're not only joyful, but they're the freest people I've known: free to be, to love, and to let God work through them. They enjoy each moment, with no regrets for yesterday and no anxiety about tomorrow. They don't have to prove anything; they work because they *want* to, not because the world *expects* it of them. To me, these people are very rich—not in material things, but in the things of the Spirit. They possess the peace and joy that come from walking close to God. Yet this route to the kingdom begins with the painful admission that we are poor and needy. This is the *sine qua non* of our spiritual lives, the most basic fact. We are to trust God, not ourselves, and God means for us to learn that.

Left to ourselves, we find this world a lonely place. No matter how many friends we have or how big our family, we feel cut off from a warmth and love we can't describe. It's always "out there somewhere" until we open our hearts and let the Holy Spirit "in here." He is a part of God Himself, and He will keep us company as long as we live on this earth.

So the spiritual life begins with our becoming poor in spirit. We place our feet on the first step of the ladder and become children of God. Though Matthew never uses the term "new birth," the Beatitudes teach us what it will be like, and it begins with "I need!"

It is neither wealth nor poverty that keeps us out of the kingdom. It is our pride, which falsely tells us we have no need. Pride lives a very narrow life. It must have all the answers and insists on having its own way. It talks too much. It has trouble getting along with people; it is prejudiced; its ego is so big, you can't help bumping into it. Pride wants too much and offers too little.

Humility is just the opposite: The humble are *not* proud. They know they need help, so they get it. The kingdom Jesus established is not to be forced on anyone, but gladly given to those who know their need and are ready to receive from God.

Humility is smart enough to know we can't know everything. It listens, and it looks at life through the eyes of others. The door to its heart is never locked. Humility is thankful for all it has, and because it has received so much, it gives unendingly.

Putting Things in Their Place

MAXINE HANCOCK

We need to distinguish between real faith in God and a mere faith in things. Turning Christianity into a "faith in God for things" is a sad, materialistic travesty of the gospel that has rooted itself stubbornly in our consciousness. Jesus told the story of the rich man whose life consisted merely in getting more and more, a man whose epitaph throughout the ages has been "Thou fool" (Luke 12:20, KJV). And while we remember well the story, we often forget its pointed application: "So is he that layeth up treasure for himself, and is not rich toward God" (12:21, KJV).

We begin to experience real riches when we stop looking to God as a supplier of things and begin to seek Him for Himself. A stanza of A. B. Simpson's hymn "Himself" tells the story of one who learned to live a life "rich toward God."

Once it was the blessing, Now it is the Lord;
Once it was the feeling, Now it is His Word;

Once His gift I wanted, Now, the Giver own;

Once I sought for healing, Now Himself alone.

It is only when I can truly say that my life goals are bound up in knowing and growing in God that I can dissociate myself from lesser, material goals and direct my energies in prayer and in life toward bringing pleasure to the heart of the One "who loved me and gave himself for me" (Galatians 2:20).

Real poverty must be ultimately described in spiritual terms. It is being "without hope and without God in the world" (Ephesians 2:12), the condition of those who do not know Jesus Christ as Lord and Savior. It was this kind of poverty that Jesus came to eradicate. Certainly He was concerned about physical needs. He fed the hungry. He healed the sick. And all without charge. He lived the simple life and shared all that He had and was with others. But over and over again He pointed out that the deep need of the soul could never be satisfied with bread alone.

Real poverty is to be without Christ or, having made a profession of salvation, not to find our very beings saturated and blessed by His presence. Real poverty is to want things—anything—more than we want God. Real poverty is to have our lives cluttered, the good seed of God's Word "choked with cares and riches and pleasures of this life," thus bringing "no fruit to perfection" (Luke 8:14, KJV).

There is, however, a kind of poverty that Jesus called "blessed." He did not consider it blessed to be cold or hungry or homeless. But He called it blessed to be "poor in spirit" (Matthew 5:3). Actually, we are all poor in spirit. Spiritual poverty is our legacy from spiritually bankrupt Adam (Romans 3). But Jesus calls us "happy" or "blessed" when we recognize our poverty of spirit and turn to God in repentance.

In the book of Revelation, letters addressed to two different churches give us insight into the real meaning of poverty and riches, not from our own, natural point of view, but from God's. To the church in Smyrna, the Spirit directed this message: "I know thy works, and tribulation, and poverty, (but thou art rich)" (Revelation 2:9, KJV). Here, a church that was suffering from deep physical poverty was warmly reminded of its spiritual inheritance. "Blessed are the poor in spirit," the letter echoes, "for theirs is the kingdom of heaven" (Matthew 5:3).

The Spirit directed quite another kind of message to the church of Laodicea:

> Because thou sayest, I am rich, and increased with goods, and
> have need of nothing; and knowest not that thou art wretched,
> and miserable, and poor, and blind, and naked: I counsel thee
> to buy of me gold tried in the fire, that thou mayest be rich; and
> white raiment, that thou mayest be clothed,...and anoint thine
> eyes with eye-salve, that thou mayest see. As many as I love, I
> rebuke and chasten: be zealous therefore, and repent.
> (Revelation 3:17-19, KJV)

To be spiritually bankrupt and physically rich was the great problem of that church and the tragedy of many of us today. There is no blessedness in that kind of poverty. But to be poor in spirit and to know it—to recognize that all of our adequacy is from God—that is the happy state described by Jesus as leading to possession of the kingdom of heaven.

Six

More Than Meets the Eye

CHERYL FORBES

How do I really see? With my eyes or with God's grace? As the discoverers of optics learned, the eye doesn't really see anything. The important part is played by light. Our eyes simply record the light that strikes our retinas.

Because God knows that our eyes are too light sensitive to survive the intensity of His face, He sends us little lights, mere hints and snatches, different angles and prisms of Himself. God shows me His face when my husband thanks me for a meal. God shows me His face when He sends a friend to correct my attitude. God shows me His face when my mother gently—or not-so-gently—chides me but still loves me. His light comes unexpectedly, unannounced. Sometimes, we must confess, we'd rather have darkness. Yet God wants us prepared for a visit any time He decides to drop in.

When I was young, my mother read me a story about a boy who could never find things, even when they were right under his nose. She liked that story much better than I did. Every time she'd had a particularly trying day with me she'd read me this story. "Don't you ever look?" she'd scold me when she had to stop what she was doing to find any socks or shoes or books or dolls or whatever children lose. The boy in the story could sit on top of whatever he was supposed to find and complain that he just couldn't see it, no matter how hard he tried. I often imagine God reading me that story. I hear Him say, in my mother's exasperated voice, "Don't you *ever* look?"

We don't look for Him at breakfast or during a business meeting or while changing the baby's diapers. God is sending the light but our eyes are fractured; our lenses don't fit. Fortunately, however, our eyes are not beyond repair.

God's light and shadow, His back parts and His side views, contain healing properties. Just a glimpse, or a hint of a glimpse, can clear our eyes so that the next time the glimpse or hint of a glimpse is a little clearer, a little stronger, a little longer. Each glance builds on the one before. After a lifetime of seeing, we're ready for a stronger view; we're ready for death. God's light—His grace—sparkles with joy and wonder; it shimmers with commitment, surrender, and sacrifice. It moves from the longest blue day of summer to the shortest gray hours of winter, from the spring of Resurrection to the fall of Advent. God's grace surrounds and envelops us; we cannot see without it.

People would have us believe that God and His grace operate in the miraculous, the outside-of-nature, so that's what we look for. But what is a miracle? A sudden, unexpected healing? A large windfall? Yes, we'd probably agree that such things are miraculous. But what about the coming of spring? Is that miraculous? Or is it merely ordinary because it happens every year? What about the first snowfall? A beautifully written story? A clean house? A job well done at the office? A superb meal? Although none is extraordinary, each has about it the miraculous.

In some ways life would be easier if God saved Himself for the big moments—the drum roll, the trumpet call, the parted brocade. Then we'd have no doubts, and He'd have our undivided attention. But who wants to give Him attention if it means jumping from the table to do the dishes or rake the leaves? If only God would work the way we want Him to—but He refuses. He's not playing hide and seek with us. That's our game, not His.

He's around when the trout are jumping on the first day of the season. He's around when the house needs to be cleaned or the phone needs to be answered or the oil changed in the crankcase of my car. God's around in every season, waiting to be noticed. He's under that rotting stack of leaves; He's peeking up through the hard ground in the first green whiff of the crocus or the last leaf to fall from the maple. Look at Him waving His arms, waiting to be called on; He knows the answers.

Noticing God's Presence

KAREN O'CONNOR

No matter how much we love God or how well we know Him, there is always more to know and love, to recognize and receive, to notice and be grateful for. Even David, as close as he was to the Lord, yearned for more: "My soul thirsts for God, for the living God" (Psalm 42:2).

His presence and His power are reflected everywhere we look—in a delicate flower, in the raging sea, in a trickling stream, on a majestic peak—in people, places, and things. We are never without His comforting arm, His encouraging word, His close and watchful eye. "I will instruct you and teach you in the way you should go; I will counsel you and watch over you" (Psalm 32:8).

If we go to the bottom of the sea, He is there. If we go to the top of a mountain, He is there. He is with us as we draw our first breath and beside us as we breathe our last. He is the beginning, the end, the author, and the finisher of all things. How could our lives be anything but a hymn of grateful praise!

In the summer of 1988, as I hiked to the top of Half Dome Mountain during a women's backpacking trip to Yosemite National Park, I had an experience that forever changed the way I view God's presence. This was a trip I had wanted to take for years, so I had planned every detail months in advance. I hiked weekly with a group of friends to build up my endurance. I learned about tents and sleeping bags and boots and stoves and dehydrated food. On the morning of our ascent I wanted to experience it fully, with no regrets.

I knew it was up to me to make it happen, to create a memory I would not forget. So halfway up that steep rock face, I did something I never thought I could do. I stopped, turned around, and stood facing out. There was no room for a false step, so I held onto the cable for support. Then I took a deep breath and looked!

In front of me and to the sides, up, down—everywhere I gazed—was a visual feast of massive pines hovering over giant cliffs, powerful boulders poised among lush greenery, and majestic peaks jutting into the deep blue sky. I could scarcely take it in. It was so much more than I had expected. I thought to myself, *This is a holy place. God is here.* I had been so caught up in the physical details of the trip that I had not thought much about the spiritual impact. But there it was.

"Oh God," I prayed, "thank You for Your presence here—in the trees and peaks and boulders, in the waterfalls and flowers. Everything I need and want—physically and spiritually—is right here with You."

Cool water from a rushing stream quenched my thirst, revived my spirit as well as my parched skin, and when boiled, turned dehydrated food into delicious soup. Fire under my miniature stove heated my food, warmed my feet, and comforted my soul on a chilly evening. And the stars and moon put on a bountiful show each night before I feel asleep.

I didn't need lovely clothes, a new car, theater tickets, or a gourmet meal. What I needed I could carry. What I couldn't carry, God provided. A cluster of boulders and rocks and a few sturdy tree limbs were all the furniture I required. A bed of pine needles made a comfortable carpet for my tent. A broad old tree provided stumps for seats, limbs for hanging wet socks, and branches for shade. Hours and hours of time to reflect quietly and to pray gave me an entirely new perspective on my life, both there in the mountains and back home.

God was here with me—in this wild place—meeting my every need and desire. How could I not notice His presence?

Dear God, I can no longer be complacent about Your gifts. Everywhere I look I notice Your presence. Today I thank You for the flowers that poke out of the ground after a spring rain, for the clouds overhead and the wind in the trees, for the mountains and rivers, and streams in the desert. How shortsighted I have been! You are higher, deeper, broader, and stronger than any mountain or sea or valley or meadow. But still these things reflect Your glory and turn my heart toward gratitude. Open my eyes to see all of this—and more.

THE REALITY ABOUT GOD

EUGENIA PRICE

Jesus Christ declared Himself to be the Anointed One sent from God.

It was on this truth that my own life changed its course, was turned completely around to face the other way. There was no fear of Dante's inferno in me. Nor was there a longing for heaven—at least not consciously. I was merely another materialistic Western-world pagan with potentially good instincts and already proven bad ones. God had no reality, no meaning, no place in my life. I had long since stopped berating Him, had settled restlessly but definitely into the sometimes dull, sometimes exciting pursuit of my own happiness, my own pleasure, my own success.

Many things went wrong, the problems piled up, but until I was thirty-three years of age, I managed to wiggle through the tight places with the financial help of my parents and with one point of comfort: Nothing is permanent but change. If things stacked up on me, I just went on, tried to ignore them or bluff my way out, consoling myself at night when I was alone with my pillow that no matter how tangled up things seemed at the moment, since nothing was permanent but change, the problems would somehow resolve themselves or just go away.

It never occurred to me to pray. I knew my mother prayed and some of my Catholic friends attended Mass regularly, but God had no conscious place in my life. Then, almost on a dare, I began to believe that God was *knowable*. That He need not be formless, vague, remote, a mere subject for discussion or heated argument, a pacifier for old ladies, a policeman for little children. I began to believe this so all-inclusively that I turned my life over to Him. "My life" included all there was of me. It included any pursuit of pleasure, my work, my friends, my good and bad habits, my viewpoint, my rights to myself.

You can be very sure that I did not make this commitment to an amorphous, vague, remote creature whom man called God. My commitment came as a direct result of the discovery of truth. The truth that Jesus Christ and God are one and the same, that if I could know Jesus Christ, I could know God. In that sense Jesus Christ redeemed God for me. I had no trust in the God of my mother or my friends. I didn't *know* Him. I saw no way to know God. When someone claimed to know Him, it sounded pompous to me, or infantile, or unintelligent, superstitious. I remember arguing many years before that I might trust God if He were knowable, but I certainly would take no mere human word for His existence. I saw no remote possibility that any human being could know God, and so I did not believe He existed in any practical way.

THE MOST IMPORTANT GIFT

How then did I manage to come to the place of giving God the most important gift I owned—myself? After reading the opening verses of the first chapter of John, I took the one leap of faith required to know God. I tossed aside my mental blocks and *believed* that Jesus Christ was not just the leader of one religious movement. That He spoke the truth when He declared Himself to *be* the Truth about God. When He claimed to be one with the Father. It was a simple as that. So simple, it is the most difficult act for complex man to perform.

I suppose it is rather obvious why we demand explanations where God is concerned. We believe our astronauts are in space, doing what they report they're doing, although not one in ten thousand of us understands one thing about the science of outer space. When we believe God, if our faith is real, it will begin to involve our very lives. Even those who proclaim *no faith* as adamantly as I proclaimed it hold far down in their hearts a secret knowledge that if they come to believe, God is going to change their way of living, their attitudes, their minds, their hearts. He will, if we give Him half a chance. He could not remain true to Himself or to His love for us if He didn't. He does not turn us into duplicates of each other, but He works steadily and loves constantly until bit by bit what is destructive in our natures is changed.

One can *know* God only in Jesus Christ. Jesus Christ, the Anointed One of God, the Messiah—the God-Man, who came to live among us in our sorrow, our grief, our hostility. Jesus Christ, the Messiah, who came to bear our griefs and carry our sorrows. The very Son of God, no *less* than God, who came to expose Himself to our hatred, our vengeance, our panic—this God is knowable.

There is little or no freedom for the Christian who dwells on God's vengeance, who conforms for the sake of conformity, who has never seen the heart of the Nazarene who healed on the Sabbath and spoke meaningfully to a despised Samaritan woman. There is no freedom for the tense, shackled Christian who thinks exclusively—shutting out one race, or one social background, or who insists upon bending others to his own legalistic approach to God. Human beings don't approach God anyway! God approaches human beings. And His heart is all-*inclusive*. He never shuts out. His arms stretched wide on the cross of Calvary are His concentrated demonstration of the welcoming nature of His love.

HE DARES TO LOVE

To live safely in the wider place, where freedom is, one must be acutely aware of the *nature* of the Spirit of the Lord, who dwells there too. God is not on the side of conservative or liberal, of enemy or ally. He is on everyone's side.

We can have no pat explanation for tragedy. Only the shallow mind would try for one. But we do have an explanation of God's nature—of God Himself—in Jesus Christ. Sin is loose in the world, war is, but it is not God's idea. Leukemia is not God's idea. Creation is somehow incomplete. The cure for leukemia will be found. Not soon enough to keep my father here to fill my mother's life, but this in no way changes Jesus Christ. He did not call the ten legions of angels to save Himself, either. If He had, He wouldn't dare try to comfort a grief-stricken human heart.

Jesus Christ does dare, though, because He has expended every effort—just think, *every* effort known to God—to make Himself knowable to us, to blot out once and for all the confusion rampant in the human race about the true nature of the Creator God. Every effort? Yes. God came, Himself, in the person of Jesus of Nazareth. There need never be confusion about Him again. Our confusion stems from trying to understand God through circumstances, through our griefs and our joys. If your life is full of good things as you read this, then God is a good God to you. But what about [a woman] in her fresh grief? Is God a good God to her? Yes, He is, because she knows Him in Jesus Christ.

There are times when it is as important to be sure that God is an *involved* God as well as a good God, and in Jesus Christ, no one could doubt the divine involvement. He is involved with us and He is committed to us. God never gives up on a human heart. God's total explanation of Himself to man *is* the Anointed One of God, the Messiah, Jesus Christ.

Our questions are not necessarily answered in words or theories. They are blotted out in the light of Jesus' involvement, His goodness, His commitment, His love—the love that poured from the heart men tore open on Calvary.

God is not the author of confusion. He is, in Jesus Christ, the Light of the world, the clarification of man's perplexities. This is the liberating news He came to bring us.

Hiding Away with Him

Settle yourself in solitude, and you will come upon

Him in yourself.

— SAINT THERESA

Nine

COME TO THE FIRE

GAIL MACDONALD

One morning many years ago, in those days when easy answers were still in my life, I found myself in an arena with thousands of other people. A retired missionary nearing his eightieth year spoke. His aged face and stooped shoulders evidenced the signs of a lifetime of spiritual warfare. Perhaps a person more than twice my age would have some spiritual secret that I could press into my own life situation. And so I strained to hear every word from this quivering voice weakened by the years.

The man caught my attention with a simple word picture as he challenged people to seek something greater. He said, "Untended fires soon die and become just a pile of ashes."

Sometimes you hear something so frequently that it loses its grip on you. Then someone rephrases it in a way that hits you like a bolt of lightning, and you are never the same. That's what that moment was like for me.

He said that the fire presumably burns in the heart of the one who follows Christ. It is a flame that cannot go unmanaged, for if it is allowed to dwindle into ashes, the outer person is destined to a life of coldness.

My life was altered by that simple statement. I'd heard the practical, personal, spiritual creed of a man who had eight decades behind him to support his claim. He proposed that we give serious attention to the condition of the "fire within." "Is it burning with force, or is it dying? Is it being fed or starved?" he asked. "Until this matter is addressed, understood, and resolved, all attempts at finding one's way through the challenges of life will be relatively futile."

For a young woman in ministry, this was an insight of massive proportions. He could not have known that his words would mark me and who knows how many others for all these years since. I've often wondered if he had read the words of Walter Hilton of Thurgarton, who once said, "Fire shall always burn on the altar, which the believer shall nourish, putting wood underneath in the morning every day, so that the fire may not go out."

From that day in the crowded arena to this one, the vitality of my inner fire has been my priority. Tending the fire within is another way of talking about being open to the presence of Christ. It is what makes me long for His likeness, offers direction and stability, establishes proper motives and responses. Here it is that the real issues of the Christian faith are thought out and pressed into action.

When I become aware that my attitude and conduct are drifting toward an un-Christlike perspective, I've learned to ask, "Have you been with Jesus at the fire, Gail? Have you allowed the fire to die down? Are there more ashes than flames?" Usually the alarming realization arises: He has been there at the fire within, waiting, but I've been a no-show.

The old missionary's picture of the fire has led me to remember that remarkable scene on the shore of Galilee the morning Jesus invited a group of exhausted, dejected, and empty-boated fishermen to breakfast. As they gathered about His fire, several things happened. The men were fed, they were reaffirmed in their relationships to Him, and they were instructed and recalled to ministry. That morning on Galilee provides a great picture of what happens—or should happen—when you or I have fire time with the Lord.

You could say that, after that moment, the fire on the shore was strangely transferred to their innermost beings. And as long as they were willing to keep that fire tended, it burned within. The feeding, the affirming, the instructing, and the sending went on and on.

Now having tested the validity of this thought for many years, I believe that every woman's life has to begin at that same sort of fire. It takes time to come to the fire, it takes effort to keep the fire burning, it takes a willingness to become quiet enough to hear what God might be saying, and it takes courage to snuff out competing sounds and demands that attempt to shorten or neutralize the effect of the fire time.

Ten

FIXING YOUR EYES ON JESUS

CYNTHIA HEALD

As I have examined my schedule, I've found that I tend to "busy" myself so that I can avoid doing some of the important things in my life that take discipline. The activities or responsibilities that I tend to put off range from writing letters to doing major projects. If I'm busy doing "good" things, then I have an excuse for not doing the important things.

I remember committing myself to a project that would take a lot of time and effort. In the midst of that commitment, though, I found myself choosing to be involved in all kinds of other activities. It was then I realized that I was doing these other things really to evade working on the project. This same tendency carries over into my choosing to have time with the Lord. I want to spend time with Him, but it takes discipline to withdraw from all the good things that demand my attention.

I think this is why Jesus commended Mary's choice to sit at His feet. Like Martha, we can allow constant busyness to crowd out the gold, silver, and precious stones in our lives. Bible teacher Oswald Chambers wrote, "The main thing about Christianity is not the work we do, but the relationship we maintain and the atmosphere produced by that relationship. That is all God asks us to look after, and it is the one thing that is being continually assailed."

To pace ourselves in our race, we must make it a priority to withdraw to replenish ourselves spiritually, emotionally, and physically. We cannot allow ourselves to let busyness control our lives so that we fall down exhausted at the end of the race. That is not freedom! There is much to do in this life, but God wants us to do all that we do in His name and to His glory. To honor that request, we must come to Him often for the inner rest, refreshment, and guidance that is needed to run our race.

Eleven

WHY SOLITUDE?

JEAN FLEMING

Solitude isn't a new idea. The first human couple walked and talked with their Creator in the Garden of Eden. At the heart of life, in all its intended fullness and perfection, man must commune with God. A growing communion with the Lord is the goal of solitude.

Like nonChristians, Christians must exercise, eat a balanced diet, and get fresh air and proper rest if they are to contribute to their good health. In addition, Christians have a secret inner life that must be cared for. Christianity is not an ascetic religion that strips the material world of value, but God does say that what a man is *inside* is more important than his outward appearance, economic status, or position in society. God looks at the heart (1 Samuel 16:7). Christ directed His most stinging rebukes to the Pharisees, who neglected their inner life but diligently exercised outward forms to give a spiritual impression.

Essential to the focused life is our commitment to God above all else. This commitment cannot be sustained unless we spend time with Him to know and understand Him. The Lord declared through Jeremiah that this is our worthiest pursuit: "Let not the wise man boast of his wisdom or the strong man boast of his strength or the rich man boast of his riches, but let him who boasts boast about this: that he understands and knows me, that I am the LORD, who exercises kindness, justice and righteousness on earth, for in these I delight" (Jeremiah 9:23-24).

Time alone with the Lord cleanses the mind. [A man I know] says that even when no particular thought or blessing emerges from his Bible reading, the water of the Word running through his mind has a purifying effect. Focusing on God also helps us view this present, illusory world with perspective by setting it in eternity and enables us to evaluate our current direction, desires, and plans. A Godward gaze often exposes error or shame in our life.

Author Thomas R. Kelley wrote, "If you say you haven't the time to go down into the recreating silences, I can only say to you, 'Then you don't *really* want to, you don't yet love God above all else in the world, with all your heart and soul and mind and strength.' For, except for spells of sickness in the family when the children are small, when terrific pressure comes upon us, we find time for what we *really want* to do." The teacher J. Oswald Sanders summed up that thought when he said that we know God as well as we choose to. Arrange your life to accommodate Him.

A TIME TO BE FILLED

How is the spiritual life formed within us? Is it a matter of discipline and persistent effort, or is it a gift from God totally apart from self-effort? Two back-to-back accounts in 2 Kings illustrate what I believe is the right perspective.

After the death of Ahab, king of Israel, Mesha, king of Moab, refused to continue supplying Israel with lambs and wool. Joram, Israel's new king, enlisted the help of Jehoshaphat, king of Judah, and set out to teach Mesha a lesson. En route to Moab through the desert of Edom, the two armies found themselves without water. Jehoshaphat suggested they inquire of the Lord. The word of the Lord, spoken by the prophet Elisha, was, "Make this valley full of ditches. For this is what the LORD says: You will see neither wind nor rain, yet this valley will be filled with water, and you, your cattle and your other animals will drink" (2 Kings 3:16-17).

The second incident involved a widow in dire straits. Her deceased husband's creditors threatened to take her two sons into slavery unless she could pay off the debt, but all she had left was a little oil. The prophet Elisha told her to collect as many jars as possible from neighbors, retreat behind closed doors with her boys, and pour the oil into the jars. Miraculously, her limited supply of oil was unlimited until the last jar was full. She sold the oil to pay the debt.

Ditches and jars—receptacles that needed to be filled. Both incidents required some effort from people, but always with the knowledge that God must do the filling. God has both commanded us to seek Him and promised to reveal Himself when we do.

Paul challenged the young pastor Timothy to train himself in godliness (1 Timothy 4:7). Paraphrased, Paul might have said, "Timothy, take responsibility for your spiritual condition. The world system you must live in will not provide what is needed for you to develop in your faith, and you cannot depend on the religious community. Schedule time for training, set your mind on the goal, discipline yourself to work at it. You must make your own environment for growth."

Our society has become very dependent on external motivation to precipitate change or learning. We think we must attend seminars and classes, and if the schedule conflicts or money is short, we excuse ourselves for not learning or growing. But a disciple is a learner. God is our teacher. He has given the Holy Spirit to indwell and tutor us. We need not depend on organized resources and experts to stimulate and nurture our spiritual life. Pray for help. Search out people who can help establish you in your relationship with God, for He does indeed use people. But if help is not forthcoming, God will assist you as you train yourself in godliness.

Henri J. M. Nouwen, pastor and teacher, wrote, "Precisely because our secular milieu offers us so few spiritual disciplines, we have to develop our own. We have, indeed, to fashion our own desert where we can withdraw every day, shake off our compulsions, and dwell in the gentle healing presence of our Lord."

After a time of family feasting, it was Job's regular custom to rise early in the morning and sacrifice a burnt offering for each of his children out of concern for their relationship to the Lord (Job 1:5). Daniel prayed three times a day (Daniel 6:10-13). For years, my friend [who is] a missionary in Korea has fasted on Sundays and spent the afternoon in Bible reading, prayer, and correspondence.

The Lord retreated for prayer daily: "Jesus went out as usual to the Mount of Olives, and his disciples followed him" (Luke 22:39).

PLANNING FOR PERSISTENCE

What established routines and choices give form to your life? Carefully cultivated habits that grow out of a spiritually developed value system have great importance. The contemplative François Fénelon advised, "You will do well so to regulate your time that you may have every day a little leisure for reading, meditation, and prayer, to review your defects, to study your duties, and to hold communion with God. You will be happy when a true love to Him shall make this duty easy."

God blesses persistence. As a result of his persistence, Jacob's name was changed to Israel (Genesis 32:24-30). The Greek woman born in Syrian Phoenicia was not easily turned aside. When Jesus failed to respond to her request to exorcise the demon from her daughter, this woman tenaciously persuaded Him to do so (Mark 7:24-30). Jesus also taught the value of persistent prayer in the parable of the widow and the unjust judge (Luke 18:1-8).

God does not respond to persistence because we have managed to wrest His blessing from Him, or have convinced Him that we are worthy, or have annoyed Him to the point that He succumbs to our demands. God responds to persistence because it communicates earnestness and singular desire. Those who care less fervently are more easily diverted and dissuaded from the pursuit of God Himself. The Lord has promised, "You will seek me and find me when you seek me with all your heart" (Jeremiah 29:13). Our God is sovereign. He can reveal Himself to anyone He chooses, but He has pledged Himself to those who seek Him with all their heart.

Twelve

THE GIFT OF CONTEMPLATION

NORMAJEAN HINDERS

The gift of solitude is one that most of us women do not give to ourselves. For one reason or another we have a bundle of very rational reasons for not withdrawing and finding time to renew our personal spirits.

At the deepest level, the entering into solitude and silence is a discipline of the spirit. It is the drawing away of ourselves into a place for reading God's Word and communing with Him. The Quaker term is called "centering down." The early church fathers called it "entering into the wilderness." Another word for the process of entering into solitude is contemplation.

Luci Shaw, in her book on journalizing, describes contemplation succinctly: "The Latin word *templari*, from which 'contemplation' is derived, means 'space'; it's also the root of the word 'temple,' which we could describe as 'a space prepared for the presence of God.' Contemplation could be paraphrased as 'spending time in inner space.' And if you are a Christian, your inner space is already inhabited by God's

Holy Spirit, so that your contemplation really does take place in His presence and with His help."

When we renew through contemplation, we fulfill the meditations of the psalmist when he said, "But I have calmed and quieted my soul, like a child quieted at its mother's breast; like a child that is quieted is my soul" (Psalm 131:2, RSV).

Thirteen

SNIPPETS OF STILLNESS

LOIS MOWDAY RABEY

A few years ago my husband, Steve, and I were enjoying a vacation in Europe with another couple. We had traded in our accumulated mileage for free tickets and jetted off for three weeks in France, Switzerland, and Italy.

Our first stop was Paris, which is a bustling whirl of activity day and night. We filled every moment of our four days there.

On the fifth morning, we packed our van and headed for Switzerland. After a scenic drive through the French countryside, we arrived at a small town bordering Lake Geneva. Our bed-and-breakfast overlooked the lake. We oohed and aahed at the sight of such peaceful surroundings after the hustle of Paris. But sighs of delight had barely escaped my lips when I shifted gears. My companions hadn't joined my instantaneous redirection and looked surprised when I announced, "I'm off!"

Steve was used to my abrupt change of pace and just smiled. I walked expectantly down the hill and toward the main street of the town. It was about 1:00 P.M. As I came to the first corner of the shopping area, I noticed that the streets were relatively deserted.

A sign on the first shop I approached explained the lack of foot traffic. *Closed from noon until three.* I tried the doorknob anyway, but it was locked. I jiggled it as if there were some mistake. Frustrated, I went to the next shop. The same sign in this store window was delicately embroidered in needlepoint, but I didn't appreciate the artistic touch. I was irritated that my plan had been thwarted.

I walked back to the hotel to snatch Steve from whatever cozy chair he had settled into, only to find him in our room asleep. Our friends were nowhere to be found, and I could only assume that they, too, were resting.

I didn't want to sleep! I didn't want to read! I wanted to be out and about, *doing something!* I walked down to the living room, out on the patio, around the house, and back to our room. Steve was still sleeping.

I finally sat in one of the chairs in the library, put my feet up on a stool, and laid my head back. One of my favorite Rachmaninoff melodies was lilting from the CD player. After a few moments, it occurred to me that the stillness was pleasant. The tension in my body began to drain away. The breeze off the lake drifted through the open French doors and carried with it the scent of lilac. *Why don't I do this more often?* I asked myself.

There was an almost audible response: *You are addicted to busyness.*

My reverie was broken as I sat up with a start and walked out onto the balcony.

When I was home, I was always complaining about being too busy. Everyone I knew did. I had tried countless times to conquer the clock with little success. But as I stood on the balcony of that lovely bed-and-breakfast, I realized I didn't take advantage of the opportunities that fell into my lap. I often felt I was wasting time if I wasn't active. While that sounds responsible, the truth is that busyness often shouts over the soft whisper of God's voice. It's impossible to focus on Him—or others—when we are always rushing from one thing to the next. Here I had an opportunity to stop my activity, and I didn't want to!

I'm not alone in this struggle. "Busyness is a curse," Sandy told me. "I think it is something that can pull us off the road, and we get stuck. At our last women's breakfast, we talked about keeping our hearts aflame on the road of following Jesus. Psalm 51:12 says, 'Restore to me the joy of your salvation and grant me a willing spirit, to sustain me.'" Sandy went on to say that the busyness of life robs us of time to have our spirits sustained, to give God room to fill us up.

There is an old Irish saying: "When God made time, He made plenty of it." Busy women rarely need more time. Rather, we need to alter our belief that we can't change. We need to bring balance back to our lives—or establish it for the first time.

Many of us are addicted to activity. We fill up every moment. Oh, we love to collapse in a chair with a magazine or watch mindless television to unwind. But the routine pace of our life is frantic. Have we become so accustomed to the busy status quo that we don't stop and reflect about how we really want to live? Are we trapped in jobs that drain the life out of us? Do we say yes to too many things?

We can only reflect on questions like these during snippets of stillness. The view from that balcony several years ago was the beginning of intentional little changes in my choices. I certainly haven't conquered the curse of busyness, but I am making progress.

Fourteen

QUIET TIME ALONE WITH GOD

KAY ARTHUR

ow important is it that you be alone with your heavenly Father? It is so important that it is the difference between life and abundant life (John 10:10). Life comes when you are born into His family, when you understand that He is the Lord Jesus Christ, and you, therefore, submit to Him and put your trust in His death, burial, and resurrection as the only means for atoning for your sin (Hebrews 2:9-10,14).

Abundant life comes as you keep on coming to God, drinking of Him, and receiving refreshment so that out of your being flow rivers of living water (John 7:38). The Father, Son, and Holy Spirit are the very source of life. Therefore, to meet in communion with Him is to draw from the wellspring of the fountain of living waters (Jeremiah 2:13). The more you draw, the more you experience the abundant life that only God can provide, for in Him alone is life (John 1:4).

Now then, beloved, how can you have an effective quiet time with your God? I believe when Christ became man and lived as the Son of Man that God not only gave Jesus to us as our Savior but also as our example. Jesus became our role model, fleshing out for us how man is to live in relationship to his God. Thus, Paul wrote, "Be imitators of me, just as I also am of Christ" (1 Corinthians 11:1, NASB).

A close and thorough examination of the life of our Lord will reveal that Christ's life was not based on a religion or on a system of rewards, but His life was based on a relationship, on respect for God as God. For though Jesus was, is, and always will be God, when He became man, He laid aside His rights as God and lived as God created man to live in relationship to Him (Philippians 2:5-8). Understanding this relationship is the key to an effective quiet time.

Relationships are not legislated; however, relationships take time. If you are going to develop your relationship with your God and your Lord, it will take time. As a matter of fact, you'll never have any depth of relationship with Him apart from taking time to be together.

Since relationships take time, you will have to determine how much time you want to devote to your relationship with your God. God leaves that up to you. He is there, always available, always waiting. Can you imagine that, beloved? The door to the throne of the Sovereign Ruler of all the universe is never closed to you! He waits for you because He values your fellowship.

Is three, five, or ten minutes enough? And how often? Once a week? Once a day? When? Morning? Evening? That, beloved, is for you to determine. Just remember, relationships of any depth take time. Settle this with your Father. Then, if it's a priority, keep it as a priority.

THE LORD'S QUIET EXAMPLE

Our Lord had approximately three and one-half years of public ministry. As you read the Gospels, it is evident that those days were filled with activity as He proclaimed God's Word to the multitudes, taught His disciples, and ministered to those who needed a physician. Much of the time, He was on the road going from city to city with no place to really call home. He was the only hope for mankind. His work was literally a matter of life and death. Yet, as the Son of Man, Jesus took time to be alone with His Father.

In Luke 5:16 we read that Jesus "would often slip away to the wilderness and pray" (NASB). Before He chose His twelve disciples, "He went off to the mountain to pray, and He spent the whole night in prayer to God" (Luke 6:12, NASB). In Mark, we read of His spending the evening dealing with the ill and demon-possessed; yet following this, "in the early morning, while it was still dark, He arose and went out and departed to a lonely place, and was praying there" (Mark 1:35, NASB). After multiplying the loaves and fishes, He "sent the multitudes away" and "went up to the mountain by Himself to pray; and when it was evening, He was there alone" (Matthew 14:23, NASB).

What priority would you say Jesus, as the Son of Man, gave to His relationship with the Father? In the midst of great demands, was it this priority of time with His Father that enabled Him to say, "I glorified Thee on earth, having accomplished the work which Thou hast given Me to do" (John 17:4, NASB)? I think so. And, beloved, if it was a priority with Him, shouldn't it also be one with you?

It is in our time alone with Him that God not only orders our comings and our goings, but He also prepares us for them so that we can discern not only what we are to do but what we are not to do. When we are with Him in the Word and in prayer, we gain understanding and wisdom that will sustain us and guide us in all other relationships. It is as we wait upon the Lord that we will renew our strength so that we can mount up with wings like eagles, run and not get tired, walk and not become weary (Isaiah 40:31).

Beloved, are you weak? Weary? Confused? Troubled? Pressured? How is your relationship with God? Is it holding its place of priority? I believe the greater the pressure, the greater your need for time alone with Him. Is it any wonder so many are crumbling under the stress and peer pressure of the world when so few have made their relationship to their Father the utmost priority of their lives?

Time is essential. Being alone is essential. This quiet time alone with God is separate from corporate worship and prayer, group Bible studies and church. It is getting away to be alone—just you and God.

From a prophecy in Isaiah, it seems that Jesus began His day in communion with God, and, in doing so, He was prepared to meet the needs of those who would cross His path that day.

> The Lord GOD has given Me the tongue of disciples,
> That I may know how to sustain the weary one with a word.
> He awakens Me morning by morning,
> He awakens My ear to listen as a disciple.
> The Lord GOD has opened My ear;
> And I was not disobedient,
> Nor did I turn back. (Isaiah 50:4-5, NASB)

BEING STILL AND LISTENING

Time alone with God involves listening! Being quiet. Being still. Prayer is vital. Prayer is talking to God even as Jesus talked things over with God, seeking His will. However, there must also be a time for listening. God has spoken to His people in many ways, yet He speaks often in a still small voice (1 Kings 19:12). He will put His thoughts in your mind, bring to your remembrance His Word, and you will hear a still small voice saying, "This is the way; walk in it" (Isaiah 30:21). And if you are quiet long enough, He will confirm the thoughts that are His, and you will know "thus saith the Lord" even as Jesus knew "what to say, and what to speak…just as the Father has told Me" (John 12:49-50, NASB). However, beloved, learning to recognize His voice will not come overnight—it takes time; it takes listening. Remember, you are deepening your relationship with your Father, and relationships take time and two-way communication.

Therefore, learn to be still. Read His Word, pray, and listen. God will show you what to do first—when to pray, when to read and study His Word, when to listen. And because relationships are not legislated, the order will vary according to your needs, your personality.

You might simply begin your day in prayer the night before. Ask God to awaken you as He awakened Jesus morning by morning. He will. He waits, longing to develop a relationship with you, to talk together daily in your quiet time until you can say with your Lord,

> The Lord GOD has given Me the tongue of disciples,
> That I may know how to sustain the weary one with a word.
> He awakens Me morning by morning,
> He awakens My ear to listen as a disciple. (Isaiah 50:4, NASB)

Fifteen

LEARNING TO LINGER

BARBARA ROBERTS PINE

Most people have heard the story about Jesus walking on water. The day it happened, in some deserted site near the Sea of Galilee, thousands of the curious and faithful had come to see and hear Him. They had mixed motives and broken bodies, and He had power. He healed them, fed them, taught them. He gave Himself.

Then, having sent His disciples rowing toward home, He somehow managed to dismiss the crowd and climbed a mountain for some private time of prayer. When evening came, still standing on the hillside, He noticed the boat bearing His friends being battered by high waves. The disciples strained at the oars against an adverse wind, says Matthew's gospel. So be it. Jesus let them struggle until early morning, when He walked toward them on the water and took care of the problem.

That is the story in a nutshell. What is not in the nutshell is the addendum supplied by the gospel of Mark: "He intended to pass by them" (Mark 6:48, NASB). What?

For hours Jesus kept an eye on those guys fighting mean winds, stalled on the sea. Apparently He trusted their survival skills; they were fishermen, after all. In fact, He planned to pay no attention to them but to pass them by. Every writer has to cut something, but Mark teases our curiosity with his brevity. *Why* was Jesus intending to pass them by? Where was He going? What did He plan to do?

Whatever the answer to these questions, in the midst of His intentions, contrary to set plans, Jesus lingered. Rarely will lingering seem to fit our schedules or intentions. Lingering results from paying attention to setting, to people, to ourselves. Beneficial lingering may require explanation, but it never calls for an apology. It is a must for real people. It is a pause, whether joyous or painful, by which we are always blessed.

WAITING FOR GOD

JANET KOBOBEL GRANT

God can be closer to us than any person, hovering next to our side, one millimeter from touching us. But we aren't aware of His presence unless He chooses for us to be.

Usually, God's presence is veiled, but we can become more aware of God's closeness as we wait on Him by remembering that He won't be rushed. Pastor and frequent conference speaker Ron Dunn says much of our praying is trying to get God to hurry up. How much better if we could pray as if we were waiting for the morning.

A psalmist captured this concept in Psalm 130:6-7:

> My soul waits for the Lord
> > more than watchmen wait for the morning,
> > more than watchmen wait for the morning.
> O Israel, put your hope in the LORD,
> > for with the LORD is unfailing love
> > and with him is full redemption.

We know two things about the sun rising. We can't hurry it, and it *will* come up. The same is true of God. He won't be hurried, but He *will* show Himself. If we could think of waiting on God as watching His sunrises in our lives, we wouldn't feel so frustrated when time seems to drag on.

But I'm more like Debbie, the child of a friend of mine. One day she announced to her mommy, "I'm sad."

"Why are you sad?" my friend asked.

"Because someone took my way, and I want it back."

So do I, and I tell God often. I must remind myself that sunrises take time, and it's my job to watch, not to create one.

Waiting typically isn't a strong trait of us humans, which may be why God seems to give us ample opportunity to strengthen that quality. Just as a child isn't served well by instant gratification, neither are adults. Patience, insights into ourselves, and space for God to work behind the scenes are all part of the payoff of waiting for the dawn.

Feasting on Eternal Words

All the promises in the Bible become your property.

But you have to find your way around in that world of

riches. You have to find out how rich you are.

— CORRIE TEN BOOM

THE WISDOM OF STUDY

JEANNETTE CLIFT GEORGE

I don't find Bible study easy. I know many people who do, and I rejoice with them in their lighthearted assimilation of God's Word. There are times when I'm preparing for my 8:00 P.M. Bible class, and at 7:00 P.M. I'm bewildered, even though I'm surrounded by notebooks, commentaries, and dictionaries. Instead of getting my notes together, I'm trying to think of a logical reason to cancel. I must look foolish to God when I'm faithlessly fuming and fretting over a lesson on faith.

Studying the Bible is a lot like eating pecans, those giant paper-shell prides of Texas. You can crack them in your hand and eat the fat, sweet meat that falls easily from the shell. Often that is how I feast on God's Word, with the accessible truths smiling up at me from the printed page. Other times, Bible study isn't so simple.

Just like eating a pecan. One half slides easily from the shell. The other half crumbles, and little pieces hide in the fragile chambers of the shell. You scrape at it with your fingernail, pound it against the heel of your hand trying to shake it free. It takes a little work, maybe even the probing of a silver nutmeat picker, but that morsel of nutmeat is worth the extra effort. It might be even sweeter than the half that fell out so easily.

Scripture provides a working recipe for learning:

> Make your ear attentive to wisdom,
> Incline your heart to understanding.
> For if you cry for discernment,
> Lift your voice for understanding;
> If you seek her as silver,
> And search for her as for hidden treasures;
> Then you will discern the fear of the LORD,
> And discover the knowledge of God. (Proverbs 2:2-5, NASB)

God gives wisdom, but we must seek it as actively as we look for hidden treasure. We will never be wise if we know only the reflection of other people's wisdom.

Eighteen

THE DISCIPLINE OF BIBLE READING

ANNE ORTLUND

*P*art of my personal notebook is for Bible study. Recently while watching a televised Billy Graham crusade, I heard the remarkable testimony of the quarterback of the University of Oklahoma's football team. Out of his mouth poured beautiful Scriptures. Then he said it had been his habit since junior high school to study his Bible each day with notebook and pencil in hand. No wonder his mouth and his heart were so of full of God's truth.

I don't know where I've been all my life, but I didn't start systematically writing during my Bible reading until recently. For preparing to teach Bible classes, yes. But that was for someone else's heart, not mine. And I must say that over the years I must have forgotten most of the wonderful truths that grabbed me at the moment, because I didn't write them down.

There's value in marking our Bibles, of course; daily I jot down thoughts and cross references in the margins. But I didn't realize, when I started making systematic notes, all the rich material I'd be adding to my store, ready to give out.

If you say you don't know how to study the Bible, don't worry. Just start in. That's why God has given His Holy Spirit to you, to teach you. First John 2:27 says, "You have no need for any one to teach you; but…His anointing teaches you about all things" (NASB).

My husband Ray's first love and greatest gift is preaching God's Word. It's certainly his passion to study the Scriptures correctly and feed his flock a balanced diet of truth. But in all his years he's never sat under expository Bible preaching; seminary helped in many practical ways, but not in learning the Bible, and he's never been to a Bible school.

So where did he learn all he knows—everything that for years has been broadcast weekly halfway around the world, and taught millions? He's learned it just the way you and I can—from digging on his own. From asking good teachers for suggestions on study books. From reading the Book itself and its marginal notes and cross references. From tracking down word studies in concordances. From praying over it.

And you know what? Whether you're a long-time Bible student or a novice, the Holy Spirit is your personal teacher, and He will grade the material for you. Each time you read it, He'll make it right just for your level of understanding at that time. He's wonderful!

So set aside time each day; have your notebook and pencil ready. Begin with one book or one section, probably something in the New Testament if it's new to you. Note the key thoughts, key words; how the passage fits what's before and after; what you don't understand, to ask somebody; how it can help your life that very day. Dig in!

You see, there are many ways to study. For instance, to study a mountain, you can get down on your hands and knees with a magnifying glass and see what kind of worms and bugs it has, whether the soil is sandy or rocky, what kind of plants grow on it. Or you can go up in a helicopter and study the mountain's topography—where its watershed is, its timberline, and so on. Study your Bible both ways. Sometimes on your hands and knees, examining one verse or one word in detail. Sometimes sweeping through it to see the peaks and valleys. You'll see entirely different things, each way.

What do you do with all this accumulating material? Have a simple file system with a folder marked for each book from Genesis to Revelation. When you finish studying a book or section, drop your notes into the corresponding folder. Gradually you'll acquire a great deal of material, amassed by you personally, on the Book God wants you to know better than any other. You'll be more and more ready to pass it on to others, which is what He's put you on earth to do. You'll begin to be engrossed in that which is truly and eternally important!

Nineteen

THE MEANING OF MEDITATION

EDITH SCHAEFFER

hat is the word "meditation" supposed to mean to us, as those who have come into communication with the living God? What does the Bible teach us about meditation? Is there a difference? Are we in danger of being drawn into something false without understanding the difference?

We need to look at a few verses to see. In Psalm 119:97 we read, "O how I love thy law! It is my meditation all the day" (KJV). Here is no special position in which to put the body, for this meditation is taking place all the day, during time in which normal daily life is being lived. Here is no empty mind, no slowed-down pulse, but a mind filled with the content of God's Law. What is being referred to as "thy law"? Not the Ten Commandments in stark outline, but the full verbalized richness of the Scripture's explanation of the commands of God.

Oh, how I love the Scriptures, the true Word of God, as I read it and think about it and come to fresh understanding day by day. Never do I come to the end of the possibility of meditating upon that. Sentence by sentence, phrase by phrase, idea after idea, and understanding after understanding drop into the fertile, tilled ground of my mind.

All the day long, as I walk in fields or city streets, as I sit at the typewriter or make a bed with fresh sheets, as I converse with professors or tiny eager human beings wanting to learn—three-year-olds with endless questions—as I work in a lab or scrub a floor all day long in office or factory, I can meditate upon the Law, the Word of God, which my eyes have read or my ears have heard or my fingers have felt in Braille. This meditation has a base, a changeless base that is as meaningful as it was centuries ago—and as true.

Then on to verse 99: "I have more understanding than all my teachers: for thy testimonies are my meditation" (KJV). How can I have more understanding as a child, as a primary-school or high-school person or a university student? By meditating upon the testimonies of God! The Bible is the place where we can have enough content to give us understanding that is complete in being true. What we meditate upon—as we read day by day and think about what we read—gives us understanding beyond man's knowledge.

CHILDHOOD TO OLD AGE

The admonition to meditate during a lifetime upon the content of God's Word is not a thing reserved for older and more brilliant times of life. Listen to Paul's admonition to Timothy in 2 Timothy 3:14-16: "But continue thou in the things which thou hast learned and hast been assured of, knowing of whom thou hast learned them....From a child thou hast known the holy scriptures....All scripture is given by inspiration of God, and is profitable...for instruction in righteousness" (KJV).

Yes, meditation—with the content of the Bible in one's mind in order to understand further—is possible from childhood to old age and can give understanding of what really is true in the universe and in oneself, beyond any human teacher.

Yes, all the day and throughout the days of my life, I am to meditate at certain times of need—even in the wee hours when others are sleeping. "Mine eyes prevent the night watches, that I might meditate in thy word" (Psalm 119:148, KJV). We are given the picture of one being unable to sleep and using that time to meditate *in* the Word of God. In a comfortable bed with the bedside light on, in the hospital ward with pain or fears making sleep impossible, in long times of waiting for news when sleep will not come, in prison where cold floors and hideous odors drive sleep away, we can and must meditate in the Word of God, the Bible. His true truth gives us what we need to know for comfort and direction.

In Psalm 63:6-7, David makes this more vivid to our understanding: "When I remember thee upon my bed, and meditate on thee in the night watches. Because thou hast been my help, therefore in the shadow of thy wings will I rejoice" (KJV). Here, if we follow David in our times of worry about violent death, rise and fall of governments, taxes larger than our incomes, we meditate rather than worry. Meditate upon God. But God is not just a word, a misty idea of our own—we have His Word telling us who He is. We read of His creation and power, we read of all He has done in centuries gone by, and we can meditate upon Him and the help He has been through the ages, and the help He has been to us individually, too. And the reality of being in the protective shadow of His wings becomes so clear that before the time is over a real rejoicing follows.

COURAGE TO DO HIS WILL

Then in Joshua 1:8, God speaks to Joshua and to all of us as we read the next day's frightening news in the paper. God has said, "Be strong and of good courage" just before this in verse 6. Joshua is faced with leadership in a very difficult moment. He is weak in his human limitations and finiteness. What is the practical admonition and advice given before the direct guidance is unfolded? "This book of the law shall not depart out of thy mouth; but thou shalt meditate therein day and night, that thou mayest observe to do according to all that is written therein: for then thou shalt make thy way prosperous, and then thou shalt have good success" (KJV).

Joshua and you and I are told to read and know the content of the Bible and then constantly meditate upon it, so that, as we speak, the true truth will come out in words others will hear and understand. How can Joshua or any one of us do God's will if we don't know the base of His law, His teaching, His character, His history? We have been given sufficient preparation to be ready to understand His will and then to do it. But what we *do* is to be action based on that which has been written in human language, understandable to brains that can think and follow sentence after sentence during times of meditation.

Doing God's will, action based on God's teaching, will follow after a person meditates—hour by hour, day by day, year by year—upon that which God has carefully given and protected so that it might be available to anyone.

Twenty

WORDS OF LIFE,
WORDS OF DELIGHT

ANNE WILCOX

She never speaks—except with her eyes. When I come to visit she shuffles toward me until we meet nose to nose. I used to feel as if my hugs were unreturned. Now I realize she hugs back with her eyes.

How I wish I knew what she was thinking! If only she could shed the handicap of Rett's syndrome for one day and tell me what is behind those eyes when they flash or when they sparkle. I would like to stop guessing and really know what she's feeling.

Angie has spoken a few words to her family: "My Jesus," and "I miss Mommy"—short phrases that reveal things I could never read in her eyes. Through Angie I've learned the value of wordless interchange, but I have also learned that language provides a unique precision to communication.

My relationship with Angie has caused me to ask, *What if God had never spoken?* What would it be like to know Him only through what we could learn from His creation, the world around us? How could we develop a relationship with Him if He had never revealed Himself with words? What level of intimacy could we experience if we had been left to play some sort of celestial charades?

Psalm 19 poetically illustrates the interplay of God's wordless and verbal communication to His people. This psalm celebrates the value of both kinds of communication, but it also exposes the uniqueness of God's written revelation.

David, the author of Psalm 19, spent many years as a shepherd and a fugitive before becoming a king. He was awakened by the morning sun long before palace courtiers greeted his daily rising. Consequently, Psalm 19:1-6 reflects the words of one practiced in observing the heavens. This shepherd poet saw each morning bursting with the nonverbal affirmation of God's majesty and glory.

GOD'S WORDLESS REVELATION

Without having to use words, God communicates His might and deity through the things we observe each day. This wordless revelation is vitally important, but it is limited.

The names for God used in this psalm expose that limitation. In introducing the creation section of the psalm (verses 1-6), the term used for "God" is a designation meaning "the Most Mighty One." In contrast, the term for "God" used in verses 7-14 is *Yahweh,* the personal, intimate name for God. Ronald B. Allen, a professor of Hebrew scripture, explains the reason for using these two different titles: "The heavens—with all of their incessant witness to God's glory—never tell of the loyal love of God. The seas—with all of their testimony of God's might—are mute concerning God's actions for Israel, His people. The trees and flowers—with all of their messages of God's wisdom—describe nothing of God's saving action in Jesus Christ....It is in the Scriptures, and in them alone, that we meet God as a person."

The message from Psalm 19 is clear. We can know about God through wordless revelation, but we know Him intimately as we have access to His heart and mind through His words. The written revelation brings clarity to the wordless revelation and provides the observer with the details of God's character and deeds.

All of God's creation is supplied with fascinating modes of communication. From complex insect dances to chirruping dolphin signals, creation is equipped for interaction. But humanity has a unique language that can express and record the nuances of feelings and ideas. God designed language for those created in His image that He might express to us the intricacy of His love and that we might understand and respond.

God's Word does more than draw us near to Him. It is our life. Humanity does not live by bread alone, but by every word that proceeds from the mouth of God (Deuteronomy 8:3). We tend to dilute this truth until someone like Anatoli Shcharansky reminds us of its reality.

Shcharansky, a dissident Soviet Jew, kissed his wife good-bye as she left Russia for freedom in Israel. His parting words to her were, "I'll see you soon in Jerusalem." But Anatoli was detained and finally imprisoned. Their reunion in Jerusalem would not only be postponed, it might never occur.

During long years in Russian prisons and work camps, Anatoli was stripped of his personal belongings. His only possession was a miniature copy of the Psalms. Once during his imprisonment, his refusal to release the book to the authorities cost 130 days in solitary confinement.

Finally, twelve years after parting with his wife, he was offered freedom. In February 1986, as the world watched, Shcharansky was allowed to walk away from Russian guards toward those who would take him to Jerusalem.

But in the final moments of captivity, the guards tried again to confiscate the Psalms book. Anatoli threw himself face down in the snow and refused to walk on to freedom without it. Those words had kept him alive during imprisonment. He would not go on to freedom without them.

DAY AND NIGHT DELIGHT

David understood that God's written Word not only gives us life and intimate fellowship, it also brings us delight (Psalm 19:7-14). It provides refreshment for our souls as well as wisdom for our lives (verse 7). It administers joy to our hearts, and at the same time it makes us true-sighted (verse 8). It meets our deepest need by causing us to love and reverence *Yahweh* forever; at the same time it gives us a righteous standard to govern life (verse 9). By describing God's Word as sweeter than honey (verse 10), David is calling it the dessert of our souls. This Word is not only our life, but also our delight.

Wonder and delight come rarely to the overfed. Our personal libraries are stocked with Bible-study helps—but we pick critically through them, taking a bit here and there to prove our pet theological positions. Rarely do we feel the passion of those famished for God's written revelation.

As I listened to a visiting speaker tell about her travels to China, this difference became painfully obvious. The church in China is desperate for Bibles. One church of twenty still anxiously waits for just one Bible to feed its members. And there I sat with one Bible in my lap, another in my purse, and a myriad of versions back home in my office.

I had to ask myself, *Do I yearn for the Word as my Chinese brothers and sisters do, or has abundance dulled my wonder? Do I give attention to the Word only from duty, or do I delight in it day and night?* Psalm 19 and others call not just for our faithfulness but for a genuine emotional response of delight.

Delight in God's Word leads to an intense desire to live according to this revelation. In order to obey God fully, we need to know what He has said and what it means. Therefore, the task of exegesis (critical analysis of a word or a literary passage) becomes serious work. We must know how to uncover the original intent of His revelation. The science of biblical interpretation must never be compromised, but it must also never over-shadow the art of loving and obeying Him who superintended each word.

David understood the importance of these heart issues and completes Psalm 19 with an intense response. He opens up all of himself to the scrutiny and cleansing of this One who has spoken (verses 12-13). Then in prayer, he yearns not just to understand God's revelation, but to be personally changed: "May the words of my mouth and the meditation of my heart be pleasing in your sight, O LORD, my Rock and my Redeemer" (verse 14).

God has spoken. We are not left to guess at celestial charades. Therefore, we have a grave responsibility to discover, through the skills of biblical interpretation, what He has said to us. But this last verse from Psalm 19 models what we cannot forget: The one who studies the Word of God must give [her] heart to its Author.

Twenty-one

THE COMFORT OF MEMORIZING

JEANNE ZORNES

y own Christian growth stagnated until I seriously memorized Scripture, in addition to reading it daily. I will be honest: I don't memorize easily. My mind is a sieve for names, phone numbers, and dates. In college I had the most creative memory devices on campus for surviving finals. Memorization is plain hard work. I do it by writing out verses on three-by-five cards and reading them over and over, trying to look less each time.

Right now I am working on the first epistle of John—three verses at a time. One of those verses tells how spiritual growth is linked to God's Word: "I have written to you, young men, because you are strong, and the word of God abides in you" (1 John 2:14, NASB). God's Word will "abide" in us when we read it, memorize it, think and meditate about it, and seek to make it true in our lives.

Jesus Christ set the example for letting the Word abide in us. When Satan tempted Him and religious leaders opposed Him, He knew just which passages to quote to disarm them. Satan and his "religious" cronies backed off, defeated by the "sword of the Spirit, which is the word of God" (Ephesians 6:17).

The enemy that the Word can defeat comes at unexpected times in unpredictable disguises. Webb Garrison wrote of such an occasion in the November 26, 1966, issue of *Christianity Today*. He remembers coming home one night from a vacation ahead of his wife and children and finding that the lights in the house were not working. Guessing he had forgotten to pay the power bill, he groped for matches and a candle. At that point he noticed an upholstered chair slashed and the drapes in shreds.

"Candle in hand," he recalls, "I moved from room to room. The farther I went, the worse it got. Great gashes in all the living-room furniture. Curtains cut in half. Bedspreads, sheets, and mattresses slashed. My wife's costume jewelry was cut, broken, and dumped into the middle of the floor. A rack of ties was cut in half. Suits, dresses, and coats and shirts were still neatly on hangers and seemed all right—until I lifted them out of the closets."

Police came and decided juvenile vandals had been at work. He called his insurance agent, only to learn the agent had failed to cover him for burglary or vandalism.

"Alone in the ripped-up, slashed-up house, I went upstairs to go to bed. With my nerves screaming, I turned back the bedspread and sheet, in which a huge X had been cut. As soon as I lay down, I felt the rough edges where the mattress had been slit."

Sleep would not come. He says, "Finally I closed my eyes and, speaking each word aloud slowly, began repeating Scripture I had memorized: Psalm 1, Psalm 8, Psalm 23, 1 Corinthians 13, John 14, Psalm 46, Psalm

90, Revelation 1, Psalm 121. I had to go through my repertoire twice, maybe three times. But then I fell asleep and slept soundly till dawn."

I, too, discovered how memorized Scripture could settle an anxious mind. When I lived temporarily in my parents' house after their deaths, memories (especially at night) seemed to loom out of every dark corner to renew my grief. I started quoting psalms of consolation and encouragement (such as 34, 46, 121, and 139) and proverbs, which I had memorized in the previous few months. Soon I experienced God's promise: "When you lie down, you will not be afraid; When you lie down, your sleep will be sweet (Proverbs 3:24, NASB).

During daytime, too, during those first difficult months of grief, memorized Scripture verses came alongside like comforting friends. I clung to Psalm 46:1-2: "God is our refuge and strength, a very present help in trouble. Therefore we will not fear." And I cherished something similar from Psalm 94:18-19:

When I said, 'My foot is slipping,'
     your love, O LORD, supported me.
When anxiety was great within me,
     your consolation brought joy to my soul.

Thinking through each phrase throughout the day was like clinging to a rock in a storm.

The more I am in God's Word, the more I am encouraged and the more I see victory over a long-term problem: anxiety. One spring I was so discouraged I was ready to write four-part harmony for "The Broom Tree Blues." My master's degree was in sight, but I did not know if I could meet the deadline looming on my thesis. The job résumés I had sent out had brought only a trickle of replies—all no. With the nation's economy getting wobblier each day, I wondered if I would find a job that would make graduate school worthwhile.

I wondered what I would do if I had no job by graduation. I was living in college housing and would have to move out when the quarter ended a few weeks away. With my parents dead, I could not go home to live with them. All these anxieties had turned into tension headaches, which made me feel even worse.

I started slipping out of bed at sunrise to jog away the tensions. One sleepy morning as I walked to the nearby track I noticed the squirrels racing across the telephone lines to rendezvous at the trees. At the track, my feet busy but my mind free, I thought of a psalm I had just read:

> For by Thee I can run upon a troop;
> And by my God I can leap over a wall....
> He makes my feet like hinds' feet,
> And sets me upon my high places....
> Thou dost enlarge my steps under me,
> And my feet have not slipped. (Psalm 18:29,33,36, NASB)

Then I remembered those squirrels and their high-wire act. They had just illustrated it!

In a few weeks—four days before the deadline—I would learn how God had been preparing the right job for me. And I would have a place to live, although "home" for a while would be a borrowed mattress in the corner of somebody's bedroom. But that lonely morning I circled the track,

I had the encouragement of the One who guides my feet in frightening places. It was as if my name were written in Scripture. Just like the story told of a Chinese man named Lo. He had become a Christian and was reading the New Testament in English for the first time. When he came to Matthew 28:20 and read, "Lo, I am with you always" (NASB), he excitedly pointed it out to a friend and exclaimed, "The Lord Jesus said this just for me!"

Ultimately, he was right.

Twenty-two

A Fresh Vision of God

Anne Graham Lotz

This past year I drove from the Gulf Coast of Florida to the Atlantic Coast. My route took me along what is known as "Alligator Alley," an unswerving ribbon of asphalt that crosses the Everglades. Again and again, to break the monotony, I tried to tune in to a good radio station, but the dial was almost entirely silent, with only two or three stations available. Because I was unable to pull in anything else, those few stations I received seemed to come through loud and clear. I found myself listening to programs I had not heard before simply because there was nothing else available. Then, as I neared the end of my journey and approached the city of Fort Lauderdale, the radio dial became so jammed with signals that it filled with static. I heard a multitude of languages and music and newscasts and accents. No one station stood out clearly. It was confusing. I would find a program I wanted to listen to, but in a few short miles it would be drowned out by other voices crowding in.

Our lives can be like that radio dial. We can be so jammed with signals coming from every direction that even when we tune in to the voice of God, He can get drowned out by other voices crowding in. If we are to hear Him clearly and loudly, there must be times of quietness built into our daily lives. I wonder if that is one reason He sometimes places us in exile, on Patmos.

It was when the apostle John was in exile on Patmos that God spoke to him, and John listened. When suffering in solitude, whose voice do you listen to? Voices from without? A professional counselor, therapist, public opinion, medical research, pop psychology, polls of human behavior? Voices from within? Your own thoughts, opinions, complaints, emotions, desires, and prejudices? Has the bombardment of other voices kept you from your daily Bible reading and prayer? There are times when I think God is silent, but in reality, He is speaking; I am just not listening.

The submission of John's will can be seen in that he not only listened to the voice of God, but he opened his eyes to the face of God: "I turned around to see the voice that was speaking to me" (Revelation 1:12).

John turned around to see the voice because he knew that behind the voice, or the Word of God, was the living Person of God. His desire was not just to hear the Word but to see and know the Person behind the Word.

When you read your Bible, do you read to familiarize yourself with the facts? Do you read to grow in your knowledge of the truth? Do you read it so you can live by and obey it, that you might be blessed? Despite these good intentions, could it be you are stopping short of the ultimate purpose of God's Word, which is to reveal God so you can know Him personally?

Sometimes, when faced with great problems, our tendency is to focus on the hands of God—what He has not done for us and what we want Him to do for us—instead of focusing on the face of God—simply who He is. Our depression can deepen through this kind of self-preoccupation. Often, in the midst of great problems, we stop short of the real blessing God has for us, which is a fresh vision of who He is. When we stop focusing on our problems and on ourselves and focus instead on our almighty and omnipresent God, our problems, as the old hymn promises, "grow strangely dim in the light of His glory and grace."

Embracing God's Forgiveness

Confession is a beautiful act of great love. We must go

to God and tell Him we are sorry for all we have done

which may have hurt Him.

— MOTHER TERESA

Twenty-three

TRUTH IN THE INWARD PARTS

CAROL KENT

T believe the greatest single cause of spiritual defeat is Satan's ability to get us preoccupied with our disappointments—especially personal disappointment in ourselves. We sin. We have a guilty conscience. We confess our sin. But our memory of past spiritual failure fills our visual image of who we are. We try to work hard to please God, hoping to somehow offset the "badness" of our "real" selves—but we fail.

Now we feel guilty. We expected to feel better. But we don't. And our disappointment leads to discouragement. So we sin again…and again. We've experienced the same cycle repeatedly. We feel powerless to change.

I think David understood the pain of disappointment. I think he struggled with guilt and felt like a spiritual failure. After he committed adultery with Bathsheba and then saw to it that her husband, Uriah, was killed in the front lines of battle, he must have gone through an overwhelming inner struggle.

David had been selected above all the rest to be the king. He was the "man after God's own heart." Surely he would have expected joy, success, honor, fulfillment, and spiritual victory in his life. So I can only imagine the degree of David's disappointment in himself when the reality of his sin caught up with him. When confronted by the prophet Nathan, David was a broken man.

Although his prayer in Psalm 51 reveals the action of confession following his wicked deeds, we can trace the reaction as David bares his soul to God:

> Have mercy on me, O God,
>> according to your unfailing love;
> according to your great compassion
>> blot out my transgressions.
> Wash away all my iniquity
>> and cleanse me from my sin.
> For I know my transgressions,
>> and my sin is always before me. (Psalm 51:1-3)

It's pretty obvious that David was feeling heavy guilt. He had blown it. His previous actions were so bad he probably would have been kicked out of my church. He might never have served in Christian leadership again in my town. He was a marked man. Adultery. Cover-up. Murder. Scandal.

In his prayer, however, we see David's open admission of the results that stemmed from his flawed belief system. He continues his confession with these words: "Against you, you only, have I sinned and done what is evil in your sight....Surely you desire the truth in the inner parts; you teach me wisdom in the inmost place" (Psalm 51:4,6).

DEVELOPING A BELIEF SYSTEM

If we are ever going to experience true spirituality, we must develop a biblical belief system that will form the foundation for unshakable convictions—no matter what disappointments we experience.

I wonder what David's myths were. He might have thought: *I am king and deserve it all. A little personal gratification is appropriate in my position.* Or, *It's easier to cover up my problems than to face them.* Or, *I know I'm God's chosen man, so my spiritual relationship doesn't need much maintenance.*

Am I being too hard on David? I don't think so. We all struggle with misconceptions that feel like truth. So how do we develop truth in "the inner parts"? Solomon gives us the answer:

> If you accept my words
>   and store up my commands within you,
> turning your ear to wisdom
>   and applying your heart to understanding,
> and if you call out for insight
>   and cry aloud for understanding,
> and if you look for it as for silver
>   and search for it as for hidden treasure,
> then you will understand the fear of the LORD
>   and find the knowledge of God. (Proverbs 2:1-5)

One of the functions of the Holy Spirit that I value most is His ability to give me a sense of uneasiness when I'm in a decision-making situation, operating with a flawed belief system. In the heat of emotion, we normally don't stop long enough to ask, "What are my firm convictions on this subject that will give me direction as I decide on an action?" We're too busy reacting and throwing a royal fit because life isn't turning out the way we hoped it would. So we automatically select an ungodly action and blame the resulting devastation on the rotten people in our lives, the "stupid" circumstance, or the devil. Satan is powerful, but I don't think we should blame him for everything.

For me, the process of "developing truth in the inner parts" begins with an acknowledgment of the Bible as the source of truth. My follow-up action must be a choice to store up His words and commands in my heart by reading and memorizing Scripture on a regular basis. (It takes more discipline than I'd like to admit.) Then, when disappointments come—and they always do—I must stop long enough to evaluate my reaction. During that brief interlude, the Holy Spirit has an opportunity to reveal truth to me.

Because of my "humanness," that pause may come after my emotional outburst. It's tempting to feel so defeated after an emotional explosion that we go back to the guilt syndrome. We think, *I've already blown it, so it doesn't really matter what my actions are.* That's a lie! We need to explore why the emotional reaction was so strong.

If I do wait before instantly choosing a negative action, I can sift my emotions through my convictions. The pause here gives the Holy Spirit a chance to bring that sense of uneasiness, if I'm starting to live according to a myth. I'm beginning to appreciate that feeling. But it's hard. It's admitting I don't have all the answers. It's acknowledging that my personal spiritual journey is still very much in process. It's sacrificing ego for integrity.

The Holy Spirit becomes my teacher and guide, and responding to His leading becomes an exciting adventure. The more I take in the wisdom of God, the more accurate my belief system is and the more often I choose honorable and holy actions.

CHOOSING A STEADFAST SPIRIT

Without a doubt, David made many wrong choices in his life. But after an intense struggle, David's ruling passion was his love for God. His action is played out in the biblical record. He chose repentance, which resulted in a restored relationship with God and a dynamic future ministry. His prayer to God during this time has always touched an inner chord with me:

> Cleanse me with hyssop, and I will be clean;
>> wash me, and I will be whiter than snow.
> Create in me a pure heart, O God,
>> and renew a steadfast spirit within me.
> Do not cast me from your presence
>> or take your Holy Spirit from me.
> Restore to me the joy of your salvation
>> and grant me a willing spirit, to sustain me. (Psalm 51:7,10-12)

There is an overwhelming joy that accompanies confession, repentance, and the restoration of close relationships with God and the people we were alienated from due to our own negative ruling passions. It's humbling. Pride is put aside. Masks are removed. Honesty replaces falsehood. That which was hidden is revealed. Without confession and repentance, restoration does not occur.

But the alternative is like a cancer that attacks the body's lymph system. You never know where the next tumor will show up. You can cover the disease up for a while, but before long it always becomes visible again. The cover-up is never worth its reward.

Twenty-four

THE BEAUTY OF BROKENNESS

JUDITH COUCHMAN

To be spiritually useful to God we must periodically travel the wasteland of brokenness. In this desert God tenderly picks up our shattered pieces and remolds them into the image of His Son. During the redesign He promises, "A bruised reed [I] will not break, and a smoldering wick [I] will not snuff out" (Isaiah 42:3). No matter how broken we feel, God won't allow the pain to destroy us.

Brokenness doesn't result just from circumstances beyond our control; we also feel pain from our sins, and perhaps this is the deepest grief of all. For me it's easier to manage external difficulties than my internal failings and personal transgressions. When I sin, I can't pass the guilt to anyone else.

Sin compromises our relationship with God and the full pursuit of our purpose in life. I'm not referring to the assorted daily sins we confess and throw away, although it's important to cleanse ourselves from these. I refer to the besetting sins, the repeated transgressions we can't release, the addictions that trouble and isolate us. God wants to use this pain to change us too.

A friend who's a therapist says when clients feel pain, it's the opportune time for them to confront their wrongdoing. Pain makes us vulnerable, open to assistance, and sick of our wickedness. It's ripe time to "let go and let God" extricate the sin that entangles us and plant our feet on the narrow path.

Once when I cried to God about chronic emotional pain, in my mind's eye I saw a heart wrapped in a network of thorny vines. *This is your heart,* whispered God. *It's dying from the sin that's choking it.* He didn't have to name the sin; I knew the disobedience that strangled my spirit. I'd love to say I immediately gave this besetting sin to God, but it took years for me to let go, bit by bit. Like people who've fought addiction, I still consider myself as "recovering." I know at any time Satan can tempt me with this sin's allure, and without God's help I could regress. So I remind myself how this would grieve God and contaminate the effectiveness of my purpose. For the love of both, I need to keep walking away from sin.

While besetting sins compromise our purpose by rendering us less effective or blocking it altogether, at the same time God is patient and long-suffering. If He waited for our perfection, the Creator wouldn't have anyone to do His work in the world. I think the key is whether we're "walking away" or "walking toward" sin. If we're willing to confess and repent (turn away) from sin, God patiently works in us amid our purpose-filled activities. "Because of the LORD's great love we are not consumed, for his compassions never fail. They are new every morning" (Lamentations 3:22-23). If we stubbornly disobey, He might set us aside for an overhaul. Think of Jonah.

Still, I offer this distinction between "walking away" and "walking toward" as a guideline, not an absolute. Who can know the mind of God? He works uniquely with each person, and often He's more merciful than humans. When I've felt battered and broken from sin, God has been His most tender. The kindness of God can lead us to repentance, yet I don't advocate testing "how far we can go" before He disciplines us. We are not to tempt the Lord our God. Remember what happened to Ananias and Sapphira.

The primary reason for abandoning sin is our access to a holy God. He is the lover of our souls, and sin hampers communication with Him. The psalmist straightforwardly explained, "I cried out to him with my mouth; his praise was on my tongue. If I had cherished sin in my heart, the Lord would not have listened" (Psalm 66:17-18). If we never found or fulfilled our purpose in life, we'd still battle sin to keep our conscience clear, to enjoy an unfettered relationship with Him. This clarity of conscience also helps us serve with boldness, unafraid of what critics might dig up and throw our way.

"Who is going to harm you if you are eager to do good? But even if you should suffer for what is right, you are blessed," Peter told the Christians of Asia Minor. "But in your heart set apart Christ as Lord…keeping a clear conscience, so that those who speak maliciously against your good behavior in Christ may be ashamed of their slander. It is better, if it is God's will, to suffer for doing good than for doing evil" (1 Peter 3:13-17).

One reason God is gracious toward our difficulties, sin, and weakness is because Jesus Christ, His only Son, suffered similar pain and temptations while on the earth. Christ's purpose was to seek and save the lost, and to accomplish this mission He accepted a horrible death by crucifixion. On the cross He bore the punishment for our sins so we can accept His gift of blood-stained salvation and exchange eternal damnation for everlasting life.

Each time I read of Christ's final affliction, I'm moved by how much grief He bore—certainly more agony than I'll face in a lifetime. The prophet Isaiah poetically predicted Christ's suffering:

> He was despised and rejected by men,
>> a man of sorrows, and familiar with suffering.
> Like one from whom men hide their faces
>> he was despised, and we esteemed him not.
> Surely he took up our infirmities
>> and carried our sorrows,
> yet we considered him stricken by God,
>> smitten by him, and afflicted.
> But he was pierced for our transgressions,
>> he was crushed for our iniquities;
> the punishment that brought us peace was upon him,
>> and by his wounds we are healed. (Isaiah 53:3-5)

Christ agonized on the cross to redeem us, but also to bring a purity of heart and a peace that passes all understanding. God is good and wants to instill His goodness in us.

Scripture reminds us that "no discipline seems pleasant at the time, but painful. Later on, however, it produces a harvest of righteousness and peace for those who have been trained by it" (Hebrews 12:11). This is the beauty of brokenness.

Twenty-five

THE POWER OF CONFESSION

NEVA COYLE

s we learn about what confession is, we must consider what it is not: Confession is not telling everyone we meet of what we have been forgiven.

I once met a woman who had a shocking and tragic history as a stripper and a prostitute before she met Christ. She came to Jesus through a street ministry—Christians witnessing and winning people to Christ where other Christians would not even drive. She longed to be "mainstreamed" into the body of Christ but felt her history must be told to her local church in order to belong. But they were not ready for her testimony. The ladies in the little country church where she settled were shocked by her story and began to treat her as though she were still carrying the effects of sin and filth. She was viewed with suspicion every time she greeted a man in the church—made worse by the pastor's invitation to "greet one another with a holy hug."

We need wisdom to know with whom we should share our past. If [we still bear] a residue of guilt or temptation, the right people hearing our story can actually help save us from slipping back. The wrong people, however, can actually *send* us back.

Confessing that we are sinners is public. Admitting details of sins committed is not a public activity but a private matter between you and the Lord. "I have been having an affair with my boss" is a confession best made in prayer with a pastor or Christian counselor. Many lives have been destroyed because the confession of sin was made within the hearing of an unrepentant gossip.

Once we experience the level of trust in our relationship with God that allows us the freedom to confess anything to Him, we begin to understand the power of confession. Confession gives us a time and place to remember a single moment when we know that we brought our sins to Jesus to be covered by His blood. Remembering our confession helps us to have a clean slate with God.

Jesus paid for our sins with His life. When we confess our sins and accept His payment for us, we accept new responsibilities. I like this quote: "For him who confesses, shams are over and realities have begun."

The realities of forgiveness and God's tender mercies are not available *in case* we sin—but because we do sin. The great preacher D. L. Moody expressed it this way: "Unless you humble yourself before God in the dust, and confess before Him your iniquities and sins, the gate of heaven, which is open only for sinners saved by grace, must be shut against you forever."

Twenty-six

THE CLEAN-HEART PRINCIPLE

CINDY JACOBS

After asking God to fill me totally with His Spirit, I assumed that my wicked heart had been changed and would automatically be under His control. I guess I thought that being Spirit-controlled would be easy, that I would instantly become like Jesus, with His heart and attitudes.

I couldn't have been more wrong! From that day on it seemed every wicked thing I had ever done began to flash before my eyes. Plus, instead of becoming more Christlike, it seemed I was behaving worse than before. The difference was that within moments of sinning I felt a deep conviction from the Holy Spirit, and my heart gradually become more pliable and soft before God.

One particular problem I had to deal with was pride. Funny how before my prayer of surrender, pride would not have been on my list of besetting sins. I was oblivious to this deep sin my life. I needed to realize there was no good thing in me! My righteousness was as filthy rags.

During this surrendering of all, the story of Joseph was precious to me.

Joseph was used by God to bring divine intervention into the life of a nation. And God surely dealt with the wrong attitudes in his heart.

The story of Joseph begins in Genesis 37. In verse 2 we see Joseph as a young, prideful teenager: "This is the history of Jacob. Joseph, being seventeen years old, was feeding the flock with his brothers. And the lad was with the sons of Bilhah and the sons of Zilpah, his father's wives; and Joseph brought a bad report of them to his father" (NKJV). Here was a proud peacock whom God wanted to use to help change the course of a nation, but first He had to deal with some character flaws.

A PROBLEM WITH PRIDE

When it came to pride, Joseph and I ran neck and neck. God would show me something about someone and I would run into that person and say, "God told me in prayer that you are filled with bitterness." Because I had not waited for God to show the problem to the person dealing with it, I caused him or her to be highly offended at me. At that time I thought the person was just rebellious and refusing to look at the issues in his or her life.

The next thing Joseph did was to wrap himself in his coat of many colors (symbolic of the anointing) and blatantly display his position. As we saw earlier, Joseph had, at least on one occasion, given a bad report of his brothers. Here, when they saw this young brother wrapped in their father's favor, it was too much for them. "So it came to pass, when Joseph had come to his brothers, that they stripped Joseph of his tunic, the tunic of many colors that was on him" (verse 23, NKJV).

This next verse is most interesting because of its symbolism: "And there was a company of Ishmaelites, coming from Gilead with their camels, bearing spices, balm, and myrrh, on their way to carry them down to Egypt" (verse 25, NKJV).

The spices they were carrying were used in Joseph's day for burial. God would use the events in his life over the next long years to bring death to the pride and selfish ambition that had kept this young anointed man from the high calling upon his life. There is a principle that is often painful to those who are full of zeal. It is this: God is not in a hurry. He takes the time He needs to build His character in us. He will patiently and methodically clean up our wicked hearts.

Most of us want everything to happen immediately, but God loves to marinate. He wants tender hearts in His living sacrifices. The problem with living sacrifices is that they want to jump off the altar. They sit there awhile and begin to sniff; after a little longer they realize it sometimes hurts to be conformed to the image of Jesus. This is the point at which some decide that the price is too high to serve Christ.

A MEASURE OF SUCCESS

God had more changes in store for Joseph as He cleansed his heart of pride. God began to give Joseph favor, and for a season things went well for him, culminating in his position as overseer of Potiphar's household. Then the finger of God touched on another area of his life—his physical attributes and abilities. "Joseph was handsome in form and appearance" (Genesis 39:6, NKJV).

When we begin to have some measure of success, it is easy to fall into the trap that says God has placed us above our fellows. Even though Joseph resisted the temptation of Potiphar's wife, he still had an enormous problem with pride. Sometimes our words betray the attitude of the heart.

Look at the number of personal pronouns and see who is at the top of Joseph's list of credits for his current position in his master's house: "But he refused and said to his master's wife, 'Look, my master does not know what is with me in the house, and he has committed all that he has to my hand. There is no one greater in this house than I, nor has he kept back anything from me but you, because you are his wife. How then can I do this great wickedness, and sin against God?'" (verses 8-9, NKJV).

Notice that the very last thing he said was, "and sin against God." One day I shared a report about an answer to prayer. It was a totally dramatic answer to a prayer I had prayed. That night as I started to pray I sensed the Holy Spirit was grieved. By this I mean I felt sorrow and could not imagine what was wrong. As I prayed the Lord gently impressed on me that I had shared the testimony of answered prayer as though I had made it happen, as though He were an insignificant part of the answer. When I searched my heart I could see how out of line my time of sharing had been. I repented and felt clean before my heavenly Father.

One great thing about God is that if you flunk one test, He will think up another. Joseph had a hard head, and God had just the solution: another stint in prison. Time went on, and God decided that it was time for semester exams. God gave dreams to two servants of the king of Egypt who were in prison with him. Joseph, trusting that God would reveal the meanings to him, asked about the dreams.

God did indeed give the interpretations to Joseph, and he saw this as his big chance to get out of prison. This statement shows his state of heart: "But remember me when it is well with you, and please show kindness to me; make mention of me to Pharaoh, and get me out of this house" (Genesis 40:14, NKJV).

Joseph missed a great time to evangelize for the God of Israel and once more did not give the glory to God. Sentence: two more years in the refiner's fire. After those two years God gave Pharaoh a dream, and the chief cupbearer for the king suddenly remembered Joseph. Look at Joseph's response this time: "So Joseph answered Pharaoh, saying, 'It is not in me; God will give Pharaoh an answer of peace'" (Genesis 41:16, NKJV).

Graduation day for Joseph: The glory had switched from him to God! God then touched Pharaoh's heart to put Joseph second in command over the nation of Egypt. When we let God strip our hearts of those things that need changing, He will share with us the secrets that the kings speak in their chambers and entrust us to intercede over whole nations.

Twenty-seven

FACING AND FORGETTING THE PAST

KAY ARTHUR

I constantly have to remind myself that *whatever happens, happens.* Once it's done, there's no changing it. No matter how hard I try, I cannot erase the past. No matter how much I might wish, stew, worry, or weep, no matter how many times I kick myself around the block, I cannot undo what's been done. If it were possible, I would undo it. But I can't. I know that, you know that, and God knows that.

We can't remake our pasts. *But with God we can handle the past.* With God, whatever has happened in the past need not destroy us.

Of course we'll face and many times reap the consequences of the past. But for the child of God there is hope. God is God, the God of all hope. No matter what has happened in our backgrounds, with God there is grace, peace, and hope if we'll run to Him and bring every past disappointment captive to faith in His Word.

Where there is hope there can never be despair. And since He's the God of all hope, the reality that our pasts cannot be changed need not demoralize and destroy us.

Let me give you a true-life illustration in a letter written to me from a dear woman:

> My mother died suddenly last summer, and as a result, so much I had buried for years started coming up—fear, pain, guilt, believing I should have never been born and that I had no right to subject people to being around me. I was struggling to deal with all of this and lost sight of God. There was a wall up and I didn't know how to get past it.

Then this woman sat under our ministry's teaching. She began listening to God's perspective. "And that wall came tumbling down," she was now able to write.

> This just showed me how much He cares....I still have a lot of things to work through, but at least God is here now.

God doesn't want you to have any regrets on the day when at last you see Him. So don't live with the "what ifs." Don't be obsessed with them. Don't dwell on them. God's sovereignty is ruling (and has always ruled) over the contingencies of this life. In the sovereignty of God, those what-ifs didn't happen. Conjecture is foolish, a time-waster. Not only that, but conjecture will also drive you down into discouragement and dejection.

Instead we can find hope in our failures. In them we have the opportunity to see and understand the redemptive power of our sovereign God—because even the negative consequences we face from our pasts are part of the "all things" God uses to work together for our good. The consequences themselves may not be good, but what they work together for is good. We must keep God's goal for us in mind, and that goal is Christlikeness.

But is all this true even if those past mistakes happened before you were a child of God?

How delighted I am to say yes! *All things* work together for good—even the things in your pre-Christian past. Although you may not know the Scriptures well enough yet to realize it, at the time you made those mistakes God had already chosen and rescued you to be His own. The Scriptures clearly teach that your redemption was planned *before the foundation of the world.* It says that those whom God *fore*knew He *pre*destined. In His omniscience He knew you would be saved. He foreknew and planned your salvation, and He sovereignly governs all of your life before and after salvation.

I love the awesomely marvelous first chapter of Ephesians. Here's God, who sees our disruptive pasts and those foolish decisions we've made—yet He allowed us the liberty within His sovereignty to make them. According to His kind intention and according to His purpose, He will work all these things for our good.

That, beloved, is why those past circumstances were allowed to seep through His fingers, for in His omniscience God knew its end result would be for our good and His glory.

How well Paul realized this! Paul knew he was the foremost of sinners (1 Timothy 1:15). As far as Christianity goes, his past record was shameful:

"I was formerly a blasphemer and a persecutor and a violent aggressor" (1:13, NASB). But Paul also knew something bigger than his past, bigger than his sin. He knew "the grace of our Lord was more than abundant, with the faith and love which are found in Christ Jesus" (1:14, NASB).

Paul could rest in God's perfect timing for all this. Paul knew, according to Galatians 1:15-16, that God saved him *at the time that pleased Him,* "when He…was pleased to reveal His Son in me" (NASB).

I'm sure that at some time or another in your life you've missed an opportunity to be what you should have been. (I know I have—more times than I want to remember.) When the opportunity came, you chose what you wanted at that moment, and yet later you were sorry you responded as you did. Now you regret it. You grieve because you failed. In your mind you go over and over what could have been different if you had responded as you should have responded.

But take a few minutes now to think about these negatives from your past that linger in your thoughts and concerns. What positive changes have they brought about in your own character and in your relationship with God and with others?

O beloved, wouldn't it make a difference if we could see that each one of our hurts from the past represents an opportunity to take God at His Word? "Be it done to you according to your faith," Jesus said (Matthew 9:29, NASB). If we have faith and do not doubt, He said we can tell this mountain (this obstacle of regrets, this hill of what-ifs) to be taken up and cast into the sea, and it will happen (Matthew 21:21).

So, my friend, it boils down to this: Are we going to believe God or not?

Twenty-eight

THE GRACE BEHIND GOD'S LOVE

RUTH MYERS

Chapters 5 through 8 of Romans have often focused my attention on a favorite theme—living by grace through faith. Both our justification and our Christian living are by grace. We do not have to balance any scales to show ourselves "worthy" to experience His total forgiveness, His warm attitude of favor, and His inner sufficiency. It's all free for the believing! For decades this truth has been a blessing both practically and emotionally, ministering to me in new ways at different points in my life.

God's love is linked inseparably with His grace, His attitude of unmerited favor toward us. Grace is the basis on which He first chose us in His love, and His overflowing grace is the basis on which He continues to lavish His love upon us.

We read in Romans 5:20 in the Wuest translation that where sin abounded, "grace superabounded with more added to that." There are no words to adequately convey the abundance of God's grace. So we can just say that it "superabounds—with more added to that"!

God's love is so great that no sin is too great for Him to forgive. We can always approach His throne of grace and receive forgiveness, whether for a large, obvious, even scandalous sin, or for any of the mass of little failures that get us down so that we think, *Oh, do I have to confess that again?* It is all grace—just as I am, I come.

One initial condition, and one alone, is necessary in order to enjoy His love. We've met that condition if we have simply opened our lives to Jesus—if we have made the simple choice: "Yes, come in and be my Lord and Savior. You died for me, and I receive You into my life." Then we're linked in a permanent personal relationship with Him through His never-deserved, never-ending love.

In no way do we ever need to earn God's love; He loves us—period. The flow of His love never stops. His love always shines forth undimmed. But our response determines whether it gets through to us. We can pull the blinds—or we can open them. We choose what we'll let ourselves be filled with, and God respects our choice. He does not force His love on us. But at all times His love flows and shines—perfect, unwavering, available to meet our needs.

We see this unchanging flow of God's love portrayed in the story of the prodigal son in Luke 15. The father was waiting for the son to turn his back on his rebellion and return home. And when he saw him coming, he didn't have to think twice about responding with fervent love. The flow of his love had never lessened, though the son had strayed to a far country and into terrible sin.

All of us need this grace. All of us have to confess sin. We *are* sinners—not, we *were* sinners. We're forgiven sinners, but we still sin. The Lord gives us victory over certain sins and enables us to grow in holiness.

But we still sin. And as we mature through the years we see shortcomings and areas of neglect in our lives that we didn't know were there. We always need God's grace.

So often, when we feel we're doing well (if we've been victorious and had our quiet time every day and learned Bible verses and been nice to our family and our neighbors), then we think, *God surely loves me today.* Then we drop into those low times—we're sure there's no way He could love us now. So at the very point where we need His love most, we don't even dare come before Him to seek and experience it. We forget that He has always loved us even when we had absolutely no use for Him at all. And He will always love us—just because.

What qualifies us to receive God's love? We qualify simply because we need it. I'm reminded of C. S. Lewis's words: "Our whole being, by its very nature, is one vast need; incomplete, preparatory, empty yet cluttered, crying out to Him who can untie things that are now knotted together and tie up things that are still dangling loose."

David understood this. Psalm 40 reveals his honest heart as it portrays the kind of person God thinks about and demonstrates His lovingkindness to. David knew what it was to be in a slimy pit, in the mud and the mire. He cried out,

> Do not withhold Your tender mercies from me, O LORD;
> let Your lovingkindness and Your truth continually preserve me....
> My iniquities have overtaken me,
> so that I am not able to look up;
> They are more than the hairs of my head;
> Therefore my heart fails me....

But I am poor and needy;
Yet the LORD thinks upon me. (40:11-12,17, NKJV)

To the person with desperate needs who is willing to admit them, God shows His love.

Do you qualify? I know I do. I qualify because I have needs—desperate needs. And He has made me willing to admit them and let Him meet them. When I fail to recognize how needy I am, He graciously works to remind me (at times in painful ways). And He renews my willingness to say, "Lord, I'm so messed up, so needy, so unable to obey You and to handle life in my own strength. So I bring my deep needs to You."

Listening for His Voice

No one is of much use who does not truly want to

learn what it means to listen and definitively choose

the life that is hid with Christ in God.

— AMY CARMICHAEL

Twenty-nine

God Calls Us by Name

ELISABETH ELLIOT

It is said that the sweetest sound in any language is the sound of one's own name. People who engage in public relations know the importance of using a person's name. Whether we call people by name at all and what name we use are deeply significant, and are often a dead giveaway of our attitude toward a person. We have, for example, a clue to the kind of relationship that exists in a marriage when we hear the partners call each other "Sweetheart" or "Mommy" and "Daddy."

I once took a little dog through a course in obedience school. One of the lessons he had to learn was to respond only to my voice. There were forty-nine other dogs and their masters in the circle, and commands were given by more than one person at a time, so each dog had to distinguish, out of all the noise, the one voice that called to him.

Sheep, too, know the voice of the shepherd, and will not follow a stranger. "He calls his own sheep by name and leads them out," John tells us (John 10:3). The Shepherd of our souls issues a personal call in recognition of our individuality.

When Mary went to the garden tomb on the first Easter morning, she did not know the Lord right away. She took Him to be the gardener until He spoke her name. That brought recognition. Instantly she responded, "Master!" And we know by those two forms of address "Mary" and "Master" something important about their relationship. In Isaiah we read, "Thus saith the Lord that created thee…I have called thee by thy name; thou art mine"(Isaiah 43:1, KJV).

How shall we hear that call? Is it likely that we shall actually hear a voice speaking our name? We cannot deny that some have. Paul was stopped in his tracks on the road to Damascus by a light and a voice. John on the island of Patmos saw a vision and heard a voice. The boy Samuel was awakened from sleep in the temple by the Lord's voice calling his name. Elijah heard a voice even though it was still and small. Some in our own day have heard voices, we are told, but I am not one of them. There has never come to me anything audible. But I have found that the Lord knows how to call us. He knows the best way to get our attention, and if we are ready to listen or to be shown we will hear or see whatever it is He has chosen as His means.

HE SPEAKS OUR LANGUAGE

A dear old Scottish lady whom I used to call my "Canadian mom" told me several years after her husband's death how she had realized ways in which she might have been a better wife. She said to the Lord then, "Why didn't you show me, Lord?" He answered, "Ah, but you weren't r-r-r-ready to be shown!"

I loved that story because it showed me her humility (such a godly lady, not ready to be shown?) and the depth of her desire to do the will of God.

But it also delighted me to know that the Lord had spoken to her in a Scottish accent.

A friend of my husband's told him how God had answered his prayer for a new secretary. A young woman called him on the telephone, and as she was talking, the story went, "The Holy Spirit said to me as plain as I'm talking to you now, 'That's her!'"

Maybe the Lord makes mistakes in grammar. Why should it matter? The point is that He speaks our language. This was astonishing to the Quichua Indians [for whom I served as a missionary]. Could they really pray in Quichua instead of in Spanish? Yes. And there came a day when He spoke to them in Quichua. We began to translate the Bible, and then for the first time some of them woke up and said, "God speaks to me!"

A SHINING CERTAINTY

It is possible, of course, because we are human, to be mistaken. I may think I have heard His voice when I haven't, but He is still my Shepherd and will call me back.

However, there are moments in our lives (and how we wish that there were many more of them) when we are given a certainty that outshines everything else. An old German hymn writer (my copy of the hymn gives only his initials "T.S.M.") described this certainty:

No other voice than Thine has ever spoken,
    O Lord, to me—
No other words but Thine the stillness broken
    Of life's lone sea.

There openeth the spirit's silent chamber
    No other hand—
No other lips can speak the language tender,
    Speech of the Fatherland.
For others speak to one the eye beholdeth,
    Who veils the soul within—
Some know not all the joy, and all the sorrow,
    And none know all the sin.
They speak to one they love, it may be blindly,
    Or hate, as it may be,
They speak but to the shadow, the illusion:
    Thou speakest Lord, to *me*.

On looking back we can tell, I think, that although many other voices called and confused us and perhaps convinced us for a time, they ever broke the stillness of that inner sea, never really reached our "spirit's silent chamber."

It is a temptation for us, as it was for my dog in obedience school, to look around to see what others are doing. Simon Peter had this trouble too, when, after that wonderful breakfast on the beach cooked by the resurrected Lord, Jesus asked him to follow Him. "Lord, what about this man?" Peter wanted to know. "What is that to you?" Jesus answered. "You follow me." Most of us will have all we can handle if we do that. We had better not get sidetracked wondering what kind of progress others are making.

Thirty

LISTENING TO GOD

CAROLE MAYHALL

She crouched beside my chair during the final meal of the women's retreat, her brows drawn together in concern and concentration. "I just have to know," she said, "How does God talk to you?"

Her question was insightful, and suddenly I was aware of using, but never explaining, that idea during the retreat. And this newly born believer earnestly wanted to know how God speaks to His children.

I thought for a long moment, then said, "For me, He speaks by a distinct impression in my heart. He's never spoken to me aloud, but sometimes the thought that He puts in my soul is so vivid that He might as well have! Many times it is just a thought or an idea that flashes into my mind and I know it is from Him."

She nodded, and we talked for a few minutes more before she returned to her table.

Later I considered her question more thoroughly. *How do I know it is God speaking and not my own thoughts answering me? Could Satan put thoughts into my head? How am I sure of what God says?* Valid questions, every one.

God is the same yesterday, today, and forever. He spoke in a number of ways in times past—through prophets, angels, and visions, through the consciences of men, and aloud as He did to Moses at the burning bush. Today, while He communicates with us primarily through His Word, He certainly isn't limited to that.

If God's thoughts toward me every day are more in number than the sand (Psalm 139:17-18) and since His Holy Spirit dwells in me, He wants to communicate with me, as any two people who love each other would.

David said, "You [God] guide me with your counsel" (Psalm 73:24). He also prayed, "Let the morning bring me word of your unfailing love, for I have put my trust in you. Show me the way I should go, for to you I lift up my soul" (143:8). These and many other passages convince me that the Lord does speak if we open our ears to hear Him.

Can Satan deceive us into thinking it is God who is speaking when it is really the Enemy of our souls? Yes, but Satan generally whispers evil things that are contrary to God's Word. And we know that God speaks only what agrees with His written Word. If I'm unsure as to whether an idea is from Satan or even my own thoughts, I disregard the message and continue to pray for clarity.

How does God speak? For me He speaks in various ways. Sometimes a thought pops into my mind—a thought so different from what I was thinking, or so creative I never would have thought of it, or opposite to what I *wanted* God to say to me. When that happens—and it lines up with God's Word—I know I've heard His voice in a distinctive way.

Many times He speaks through a verse of Scripture. As I'm reading, one verse will seem to reach out, grab me by the shoulders, give me a little shake, and command, "Take special note!" But often God and I have quite a conversation together simply by my hearing His still, small voice speaking quietly through an impression to my inner self. What an encouragement it is when I tell Him, "I love You, Lord," and I hear His whisper, "And *you* are my beloved."

I pray frequently that I'll hear His voice more often and more clearly. When I don't, I know He hasn't stopped speaking; rather, I have stopped listening.

Thirty-one

HEARING GOD IN HIS WORD

MARTHA THATCHER

For what are we listening when we open our Bibles? Perhaps you have had the experience, as I have, of wishing the words on the page would suddenly come alive. Yet you've been discouraged to find that despite your earnest intention, they remained simply printed words.

Why does this experience of lifelessness occur? Assuming we have dealt with any sin of which we are conscious, made ourselves available to God in His Word, and come trusting His Person, we must give our attention to the focus of our listening.

Herein lies the root of our discouragement: We are listening for some-*thing*, not Some*one*. This deviation of focus is subtle but pivotal. On it hinges our communication with our Lord, for it not only hinders our hearing, it also demotivates our praying. Who is excited about pouring his or her heart out to a God who seems silent? Without the right focus, listening degenerates to polite (if frustrated) attention, and praying becomes dry duty.

See if you recognize any of these responses: "I'm not getting anything out of my quiet time (Bible study) lately." "I wish the Bible seemed more relevant to me—it's so dry and obscure most of the time." Neither of these concerns is wrong, but they reflect the deviation of focus that is crucial. These concerns are issue-centered, not God-centered. They focus on what God is saying, without a prior focus on God Himself.

Issue-centered listening is a perilous endeavor. By nature it is both selective and pressured. Often what results from such listening is a misuse of Scripture, an attempt to use one verse as a simple answer to a complex situation, an effort to justify selfish preference with Bible quotes, or a frantic grasping of a few words as a direct cue from God in a situation we want to resolve quickly.

This kind of listening commits the sin of treating God as a means, not an end. With such a frame of mind, whether we realize it or not, we are using God to try to get what we think we need. Instead, God calls us to listen to Him, to seek His face; He will take care of our needs. Matthew 6:33 echoes that very call: "But seek first his kingdom and his righteousness, and all these things will be given to you as well."

OUR PRIMARY FOCUS

Our primary focus in listening must be God Himself. We must listen primarily for a person—the Person—not a voice, a word, or a relevant truth. I say primarily, because although hearing God's voice and Word on relevant issues is an indispensable prerequisite to obedience, unless we are listening for God Himself, it is highly unlikely that His voice will ever be distinguished from the clamor around us.

And so, as we open the Word, our hearts should cry out with David,

"Your face, LORD, I will seek" (Psalm 27:8). We can devise questions that will help keep this focus: What is revealed about *God* in these verses? What do I see of *God's* heart, thoughts, plans, intentions, character, work among men in this passage? How is *God* responding in this event or circumstance?

When we seek God in His Word, we will find ourselves hearing Him. We will know Him better and better and, in that context, the truths He reveals, the principles He shares, the insights He gives will become profoundly meaningful to our everyday existence. To seek truths and insights without a focus on God Himself is not to commune with a Person who will speak to us, but to collect ideas that will be at best temporarily helpful, at worst obscure and irrelevant. As we look into the face of God, the words God has for us will take on the perspective He intends for our current situation.

TRAINING OUR EARS

How does this work out practically? In Job's trauma-laden life we see this shift of focus enacted in painful reality. Job is a believer. He prays and follows God. But when tragedy strikes like the staccato round of a machine gun, he searches vainly for an explanation. He cannot hear God. And what he believes about God, though true, certainly doesn't help him much. His friends heap more advice and information on him, which only makes matters worse. Job still does not hear God.

Then, thirty-eight chapters into Job's excruciating torment, God speaks. The Lord reveals Himself to Job, exposing His character, His heart, His thoughts, His ways with humanity. For the first time, Job shifts his eyes from what has happened to him to look fully at his God. Job is no longer listening for an answer, an explanation, a statement of just how God relates to the mess in which he agonizes. Now he is listening to God. He is no longer the bewildered sheep, stumbling about in search of the path, fearful and despairing. Now he is the weary, humbled, and comforted sheep, gratefully enraptured at the sight of his Shepherd's face as he describes the change of focus he has undergone: "My ears had heard of you but now my eyes have seen you" (Job 42:5).

Our private training takes place in the presence of God, through the Word of God. It is here that we learn to hear the voice of God as we keep our eyes on His Person. With our focus on Him, our minds willing and our ears open to hear His loving voice—even if it directs us to painful change—we will be taught by God's Spirit.

In this context, God will direct His living Word to our need and understanding. Our minds will grasp the ways in which God's Word relates to the current concerns of our lives, and we will sense His specific instruction. Isaiah reminds us that "whether you turn to the right or to the left, your ears will hear a voice behind you, saying, 'This is the way; walk in it'" (Isaiah 30:21). Then, in excited surprise, we will exclaim, "God has spoken to me!"

Thirty-two

Whatever Darkness I'm In

LOIS WALFRID JOHNSON

y foot slid on the clay bank, dislodging a stone that tumbled down the steep path ahead of me. Pausing for a moment, I clung to the trunk of a small tree with one hand.

Ahead of me, my husband moved on, and so did I—half walking, half sliding, until reaching a ledge partway down the cliff. Before us yawned the entrance to a cave we had discovered a month before. Now we were back with flashlights and friends, ready to explore. Entering the wide, high room that offered coolness after the summer day, we followed the beam of my husband's flashlight—tracing his steps as the passage snaked back into a limestone cliff. Crouching low in spots, we brushed against narrowing walls, always following the light, until we could go no further.

No matter how small a beam is, it leads me if the way is dark. Long ago Christ promised, "I am the light of the world....Whoever follows me will have the light of life and will never walk in darkness" (John 8:12, TEV). As I walk in faith, God gives the certainty I will be led if I ask.

While not attempting to limit God, I find it helpful to be aware of different ways He moves. Some think the only answer is yes. While He has abundantly supplied me with that kind of reply, I have prayed long enough to be grateful for the times He answers no. He also responds in a way that indicates, "Wait for personal growth or better timing," or, on occasion, "Get up and get going, Lois."

As I seek God's will or tell Him my needs, I discover how He responds.

• *God's written Word.* Often God's answers come from more than one source; if so, those sources should harmonize. The most important of these is His written Word. Answers to prayer are either found in Scripture or are consistent with the truths taught there.

Occasionally I'm asked, "How did you get that answer?" At times I do need certain passages of reassurance and turn to favorite verses. Yet as a regular Bible reader, I seek answers from daily devotions. By praying, "Lord, what do You want me to do about this situation or that problem?" I prepare my heart for His response.

More than twenty years ago, I received a diagnosis of life-threatening breast cancer. When the way ahead seemed extremely dark, the Lord strengthened me with numerous passages of guidance. Eight months after my mastectomy, the oncologist told me he would change my chemotherapy to a different combination of drugs. I had mixed reactions to this news—partially good, for he held out two rainbows at the end. Doctors had found the program offered better results than the regimen I had been on. Also, if I did not suffer a recurrence in the meantime, I might finish treatments at the end of an additional ten months.

For the first time I had been given the hope I might go off chemotherapy instead of being on it the rest of my life. Even so I dreaded the unknowns, the injections, the possibility of additional side effects. The morning I was to begin the new treatment, my reading included Psalm 27:13-14: "I believe that I shall see the goodness of the Lord in the land of the living! Wait for the Lord; be strong, and let your heart take courage; yea, wait for the Lord!" (RSV). God reassures me this way when I need it, giving encouragement that I am still following the light.

• *An open door or blockage.* By committing everything, I give God the opportunity to answer my prayers in a second way—through the sense of an open door or blockage. When offering the situation to Him, I still know the certainty of being led, even if for a time I experience a strange hindrance, with nothing falling in place. Acts 16:6 offers the scriptural basis for this: "And they [Paul and Silas] went through the region of Phrygia and Galatia, having been forbidden by the Holy Spirit to speak the word in Asia. And when they had come opposite Mysia, they attempted to go into Bithynia, but the Spirit of Jesus did not allow them" (RSV).

Yet sometimes apparent failure proves to be eventual success. Because of the blockage Paul and Timothy experienced and accepted, they went into Troas and then Macedonia. Their journey changed history, affecting the rest of the world. In being obedient to God's call, they began missionary journeys in Europe.

When wondering if my prayers are being answered, I look for coincidences that come after specific requests. If God wants me to go ahead, He arranges circumstances so I can act on them. They might not be as dramatic as the wind blowing all night, creating a dry path for the Israelites to cross the Red Sea. Yet they will be just as real, for God still actively leads.

• *Words or actions of other people.* In times of darkness I pray with trusted Christian friends who hold the flashlight for me, offering the light of Jesus. When seeking help in making a decision, I pray, "Lord, give me counselors or Christian friends who will, to the best of their ability, look at things from Your viewpoint." At crucial times I have been offered much advice, even without asking for it. In those moments my spiritual pores need to be open to God so I sense His Spirit speaking when the right counsel is given. When I am open, the Spirit takes what is true and sends it home, piercing the innermost part of my being. The sword may be one of conviction, involving confession or forgiveness. Yet that sword may also provide a thrust of encouragement, creating in me the sureness that says, "Yes, that's right."

When Christ spoke to two men on the road to Emmaus, they did not recognize Him. Afterward they acknowledged the truth of His words by asking themselves, "Wasn't it like a fire burning in us when he talked to us on the road and explained the Scriptures to us?" (Luke 24:32, TEV).

If it's important I know something, God usually speaks to me in more than one way. Using different sources or people unrelated or unknown to each other, the Spirit verifies His leading, giving almost exactly the same message. Within two weeks of my surgery for breast cancer, I received mail from all parts of the United States. Within three weeks cards came from other countries. The notes meaning the most were ones in which people had written a verse. Some passages were offered more than once. Scriptures not frequently used in connection with illness particularly interested me. Soon I noticed a definite pattern. From people geographically spread far apart came a common message of encouragement.

None of these knew I was asking, "Lord, am I going to live, or do You want me to get ready to die?" Certainly, it wouldn't be hard to guess I might be asking that question. But the overall effect of receiving a certain kind of verse was to believe God wanted me to continue to pray for healing. And I was healed!

If God truly speaks through people, their words will be consistent with overall teachings of Scripture. No one should take a verse out of its setting, using it in a way that denies basic teachings of the Bible. Because people say to me, "The Lord told me this," does not mean I must accept their revelations without using the intellect, discernment, and common sense God gave me. In dealing with advice or encouragement offered by others, I should experience a corresponding certainty. If God wants me to know something, He reveals it to me and uses other people to confirm it.

Thirty-three

THE HARMONY OF HIS VOICE

HANNAH WHITALL SMITH

e come to the question as to how God's guidance is to come to us, and how we shall be able to know His voice. There are four ways in which He reveals His will to us: through the Scriptures, through the convictions of our own higher judgment, through providential circumstances, and through the inward impressions of the Holy Spirit on our minds. When these four harmonize, it is to say that God speaks.

For I lay it down as a foundational principle, which no one can gainsay, that of course His voice will always in be in harmony with itself, no matter in how many different ways He may speak. If God tells me in one voice to do or to leave undone anything, He cannot possibly tell me the opposite in another voice. If there is a contradiction in the voices, the speaker cannot be the same. Therefore my rules for distinguishing the voice of God would be to bring it to the test of this harmony.

The Scriptures come first. If you are in doubt upon any subject, you must, first of all, consult the Bible about it and see whether there is any law there to direct you. Until you have found and obeyed God's will as it is there revealed, you must not ask nor expect a separate, direct, personal revelation. A great many fatal mistakes are made in the matter of guidance by overlooking this simple rule. Where our Father has written out for us a plain direction about anything, He will not, of course, make an especial revelation to us about that thing. And if we fail to search out and obey the Scripture rule, where there is one, and look instead for an inward voice, we shall open ourselves to delusions, and shall almost inevitably get error.

Second, our own judgment. Some may say, "I thought we were not to depend on our human understanding in divine things." I answer to this that we are not to depend on our unenlightened human understanding, but upon our human judgment and common sense enlightened by the Spirit of God. That is, God will speak to us through the faculties He has Himself given us, and not independently of them, so that just as we are to use our outward eyes in our outward walk, no matter how full of faith we may be, so also we are to use the interior eyes of our understanding in our interior walk with God.

The third test is that of providential circumstances. If a "leading" is of God, the way will always open for it. Our Lord assures us of this when He says, in John 10:4, "And when he putteth forth his own sheep, he goeth before them, and the sheep follow him for they know his voice" (KJV). Notice here the expressions "goeth before," and "follow." He goes before to open a way, and we are to follow in the way thus opened. It is never a sign of divine leading when the Christian insists on opening his own way and riding roughshod over all opposing things. If the Lord "goes before us," He will open the door for us, and we shall not need to batter down doors for ourselves.

The fourth point I would make is this: Just as our impressions must be tested by the other three voices, so must these other voices be tested by our inward impressions; and if we feel a "stop in our minds" about anything, we must wait until that is removed before acting. A Christian who had advanced with unusual rapidity in the divine life gave me, as her secret, this receipt: "I always mind the checks." We must not ignore that voice of our inward impressions and not ride roughshod over them.

Thirty-four

SPEAK, LORD

ELIZABETH SHERRILL

He was a circuit judge, tramping endlessly between district seats: from Bethel to Gilgal to Mizpah, then back to his wife and children in Ramah. Times were hard in Samuel's day. The Philistines, supplied with arms by Egypt, had driven the dispirited Israelites from the good bottomland; all they retained of the Promised Land were these rocky and infertile hills where Samuel walked.

His route took him regularly past the ruins of Shiloh, the town where he lived as a boy, razed to the ground during the Philistine occupation. That heap of rubble there had been the temple where the ark of the Lord had once been kept. There was the gate—the only part of the wall still intact—where the old priest Eli used to sit. Here Samuel's astonishing career had begun.

The sunburnt man trudging these stony hills was far more than an arbitrator of boundary disputes between farmers. He was a patriot who had roused his countrymen to throw off the Philistines' yoke. He had summoned Israel away from idol worship, anointed kings, and paved the way for the glorious period of Jewish history soon to follow.

It all began here in Shiloh early one morning before daylight, when twelve-year-old Samuel learned the secrets of hearing God. The youngster was awakened by a voice in the cold predawn. Jumping from his mat on the floor, he ran to Eli's side: "Here I am, for you called me."

But Eli had not called. Samuel returned to his pallet and the voice called again. Once more Samuel went to see what Eli wanted; once more he was told to go back to sleep. Yet a third time the urgent voice summoned him; still it never entered Samuel's head that he could be hearing God.

To me, this is an immensely reassuring story. I tend to imagine that the spiritual giants of the past had an easier time discerning God's voice than I do. But they were as hindered by their preconceptions as we are. If we do not—not *really*—expect God to speak, we will miss Him when He does.

"Samuel! Samuel!" called the voice in Shiloh. In the Bible, a person's name stands for his uniqueness, the essential qualities that make him himself and no one else. God's word for the present moment always has a name attached. It is not only *logos*—true for all time and people—but *rhema*, true today for you in particular. It will speak in terms of what interests, distresses, frightens, or delights you at this moment; it will have your name on it.

To believe that God speaks, and speaks to you personally, is still not the whole story. When Samuel appeared a third time at Eli's bedside, the old priest realized that the lad was hearing God.

"If it happens again," he told the boy, "reply, 'Your servant is listening!'" Your servant, ready and waiting to do Your will—as soon as he knows what it is! When we present ourselves to God as servants, we offer our obedience, not our opinions. In Samuel's own view, years later, Jesse's son Eliab was the right choice for king of Israel. But God, whose servant Samuel was, ordered him to anoint Jesse's youngest son, David. We engage to carry out God's design; only then does He unfold it for us.

"Your servant hears" was easy enough for young Samuel to say, but the message that followed pinned him to his mat in consternation. Could he be hearing right? Was he really to tell his venerable and beloved master that he and his entire family were going to be destroyed by God? The boy obeyed: He passed on the fateful message. He must have remembered this moment of difficult obedience years afterward when he was instructed by the same divine voice to go to King Saul—Saul with his hair-trigger temper and killing rages—and inform him that God was wrenching the kingdom of Israel out of his hands.

Lord, let me learn with faithful Samuel to say, "Your servant hears."

Trusting God and His Ways

We may be certain, more certain than we are that the

sun will rise tomorrow, that God's will is the most

lovely thing the universe contains for us.

— HANNAH WHITALL SMITH

Thirty-five

THE ONE THING NECESSARY

ELISABETH ELLIOT

A dear woman in Hungary has chosen the simple way over the complex. She writes, "My longing for a husband is there, but I have offered it up to the Lord. Often I imagine a single future for myself. In fact, the presence of a man in my life would be an unexpected gift. Thank you for praying for me. I wouldn't like to put my own imagined happiness before God's greater glory."

Acceptance of the will of God is always a simple thing, though for us who are yet far from sainthood it is often not an *easy* thing. Our lives are still complicated, our aims mixed, our vision clouded. No wonder Jesus told us to consider the birds and lilies. We spend much time in talk, we write books about deep things, but we miss seeing God's little chickadee as he flits cheerily in the snow-laden evergreen, finding the seed God has put there for him, doing nothing but what God made him to do.

I would like to do nothing but what I was made to do. I am sure this is what God intends. How shall I know what that is except in quietness?

How shall I listen if I am full of talk? I must cease the rehearsal of personal wants and feelings, willingly release things that seem important but in fact have nothing to do with my true goal. The itch to know and to have and to be anything other than what God intends me to know, to have, and to be, must go.

This is a far cry from quietism. It may sound to some like an indolent and sluggish way of life, mere spiritual torpor, perhaps even the Eastern ideal of absence of desire. "And yet I do speak words of wisdom to those who are ripe for it," wrote Paul, "not a wisdom belonging to this passing age, nor to any of its governing powers, which are declining to their end; I speak God's hidden wisdom, his secret purpose framed from the very beginning, to bring us to our full glory" (1 Corinthians 2:6-7, NEB).

If we truly believe that God wants to bring us to our full glory, we will long increasingly to unite our will with His. It is in exact proportion as we do this that we will find happiness here on earth.

"This one thing I do" was Paul's motto. He was always moving "with hands outstretched to whatever lies ahead" (Philippians 3:14, Phillips)—straight for the goal, to fulfill his calling. But what a great number of apparent setbacks he suffered! Prison, for example. When it was possible to avoid prison Paul avoided it. (Let no one take it that we are never to fight wrongs or disabilities or setbacks.) When there was no way to avoid it, he regarded it as no setback at all. He wrote to the Ephesians that they were not to lose heart because of this. In fact, they ought to feel honored, for he had been entrusted the grace of carrying the gospel to the Gentiles. It would cost him something, but his being bound in prison chains did not in the least frustrate the purpose of God.

Do we give thought to our vital part in the unfolding of the complex wisdom of God's timeless purpose? While angels wait and watch, our part is to be simple—simply to trust, simply to obey, and leave the complexities to the Engineer of the universe.

Nothing would upset our equilibrium if our goal were pure and simple, as was Paul's. When, as a prisoner, he was taken on a voyage across the Adriatic Sea, an angel stood beside him and told him not to be afraid, in spite of winds of hurricane force, for God would spare his life and the lives of all on board. Paul cheered his guards and fellow passengers with the good news, but the bad news was that they would have to run aground on some island (Acts 27:22-26).

It would seem that God might have saved the ship, too, and spared them the ignominy of having to make it to land on the flotsam and jetsam that was left. The fact is He did not, nor does He always spare us. Running aground is not the end of the world—sometimes it fits in very neatly with God's running of the world. It certainly helps us make the world a bit less appealing to us, drawing our attention to a far better one.

Thirty-six

THE JOY OF OBEDIENCE

CATHERINE MARSHALL

It took my friend Pat Baker several years to conquer her cigarette habit. But finally breaking the habit was the least of her rewards. She was given insights about her own personal motivations, about the difference between real and counterfeit sacrifice, and how important it is to let God design the blueprint for obedience rather than trying to fabricate it ourselves.

After many tries, Pat had at last achieved a four-month conquest of the smoking habit. The victory had come through a simple step of obedience. For weeks Pat had been feeling God's inner "Stop" each time she reached for a pack of cigarettes. There came a day when she said yes but added, "If I'm going to have to quit, You'll have to do this for me." Lying on the dresser before her was a pack of cigarettes. Deliberately she left them there. Every time she was tempted to pick one up, she would think, *If this were my idea to stop, I'd already have a cigarette in my mouth by now. But it's just not me at all.*

She found it exhilarating—the most joyful experience of her life. Then one evening she and her husband, Dick, had an argument. In a spirit of rebellion, Pat fled the house and drove around town trying to dispel her anger. All at once she found herself reaching for a pack of cigarettes her husband had left on the front seat. Even as she did so, she was saying on the inside, *Lord, I know You've told me to stop. And I really will stop—but not quite yet.*

For a year after the argument with her husband, Pat found herself waging a losing battle in her struggle with tobacco. She asked prayers from all and sundry friends. Some of them suggested that one way of tackling the problem was to probe why she had started smoking in the first place. Yet Pat could find no answer to the question.

At last she got to that point of desperation. "O Lord, I want to be free. I really do. And I won't take the cigarettes back this time." There was no immediate answer.

Then one Sunday afternoon she felt as if she was coming down with a cold. She decided on a nap. When she awakened she instantly recognized there was something not of herself in the clear thought in her mind: *Get up. Get dressed. Go down to the Bethany Church.*

Pat was inclined to argue, "Lord, that's a wild church. I'm an Episcopalian. I've never been in that kind of place." Then more humbly: "Lord, if this is really You and this is what I'm supposed to do, would you please let Dick agree to it?"

Ordinarily her husband would say in a situation of this kind, "Don't be ridiculous. You've been out three nights this week. Be sensible and go back to bed."

This time, however, when she told him of the strange nudging, he answered, "Go ahead. I think you should."

AT THE WILD CHURCH

When Pat got to the church she found that some sort of evangelistic services were going on. She slipped into the back hoping she wouldn't be noticed.

Then the preacher's words caught her attention. He was speaking about Cain and Abel, and about Abel's "more excellent sacrifice" (Hebrews 11:4, KJV).

"Perhaps," the young preacher said, "Cain never had liked the idea of killing innocent little lambs as a sacrifice to Jehovah. Why would Jehovah ask them to do that? Wouldn't it be better to wait until he understood why, and then obey? Meanwhile, if God wanted a sacrifice, how about that beautiful mound of fruits and vegetables he had grown! Surely Jehovah would like those!

"You see, the problem with Cain," the young preacher summarized, "was that he was offering a sacrifice all right—one that he had thought up, but not the sacrifice God had asked for."

Sitting there listening, Pat thought of all her multitudinous church and civic activities, of her generous giving of time and money, of her sacrifices during Lent. But the clear counterthought came to her: *None of this is any good unless you do the particular thing I'm asking you to do.*

Now the evangelist was giving an altar call, but it wasn't the usual one. "All those," he said, "who came here expecting God to do something for them, come forward to receive it."

That sounded the right note to Pat. She knew that being there hadn't been her idea in the first place. *But,* she struggled with herself, *I'm just not going down there. I know that young man will shout like those other evangelists do. Lord, do they have to be so loud about it?*

Moments later she was astonished to find herself kneeling at the altar rail. The evangelist made his way to her first. Without saying a word, he knelt quietly on the other side. Pat looked across the rail at him, surprised at his quietness. Finally he said, almost whispering, "The Holy Spirit never gives one of us a message for another person in order to hurt or embarrass them. The message is given to help another. Do you understand that?"

"Yes, I do," Pat replied, marveling at the way the young minister was speaking directly to her thoughts.

"Well, God is ready to deal with you about your problem with nicotine." Pat stared at him in astonishment. How could he possibly know that? She listened wide-eyed as he began telling her when and why she had started to smoke. Then the evangelist told Pat how to get free: "If you will resist the nicotine for three days, the Lord will do the rest. At the end of that time, He promises to reveal something of the particular work He's calling you to do."

As she drove home that night Pat thought, *Well, I suppose I can do anything for three days.* But she was to find even three days much more difficult than it had been the first time. Now it was a moment-by-moment battle.

On the third day, a friend whose marriage was in trouble came to thank Pat for helping her find her way out of darkness several weeks before. Immediately, Pat realized that she had allowed her bondage to cigarettes to interfere even with helping other people. The impact of her friend's gratitude brought Pat tears of remorse, followed by a surge of joy and a strong resolve that bolstered her resistance.

OBEDIENCE BEFORE KNOWLEDGE

The battle of the cigarettes is four years behind Pat now. Depending on the Lord (instead of cigarettes) in moments of friction and stress has brought Pat not only joy, but a steady stream of deepening insights to help other people with their problems.

So we're back full circle to the only basis there is for obedience—love and trust. It may seem hard to be asked to have this kind of confidence before we have had personal experiences of God. But He also helps us out of that dilemma. The moment we "purpose in our heart" to obey Him, at that instant He comes to help us. His incomparable gift is the ability to obey, to move out into what usually looks like uncharted and dangerous country.

That's the way it was for Abraham long ago. The Lord had told him to uproot himself and his family: "Get thee out of thy country, and from thy kindred...unto a land that I will shew thee...and I will bless thee...and thou shalt be a blessing" (Genesis 12:1-2, KJV).

There was the word of command. There was the promise of blessing. There was no option to ask "Why?" or "Please explain everything to me." Always and always the understanding comes after the obedience.

So Abraham obeyed. "He went out, not knowing whither he went" (Hebrews 11:8, KJV). He did not need to know because God knew. And the result of this "blind" obedience has blessed uncounted millions down all the generations.

SACRIFICING OUR ISAACS

KAREN BURTON MAINS

There is perhaps no more moving scriptural account than the one from Genesis 22, where Abraham hears the voice of God calling to him, "Abraham! Take your son, your only son, Isaac, whom you love, and go to the region of Moriah. Sacrifice him there as a burnt offering on one of the mountains I will tell you about" (verse 2). What a momentous message for any parent to hear!

Scripture is filled with passages of drama, but none more portentous than this: "Early the next morning Abraham got up and saddled his donkey. He took with him two of his servants and his son Isaac. When he had cut enough wood for the burnt offering, he set out for the place God had told him about" (verse 23).

I can't read this passage without marveling at Abraham's obedience. Commentators often remark about his faith—he responds to Isaac's question about the absent lamb by saying, "God himself will provide the lamb for the burnt offering, my son" (verse 8). But I wonder if at that moment

Abraham's faith wasn't numb. Mine would have been. I suspect, at least at certain moments in this journey into sacrifice, that it was sheer blind obedience that propelled the father.

And I understand why God waited for old age to test the faithfulness of Abraham's love. It takes a lifetime of practice to offer up to God what we cherish most.

A NECESSARY OFFERING

At different journeying posts in each of our lives, God asks us to give up to Him the current object that we love. He tests our willingness; He tests our obedience.

It's important for parents to walk to this spiritual altar, to offer their children back to the Lord. For many of us, this begins when they are infants. We give them to God in a dedicatory service or through a christening ceremony. We give them up to the Lord, sometimes on that first day of school watching them walk away from home, looking so small, so vulnerable before the enormous destructive forces that range the world. We suddenly realize we are not all-powerful but are dependent upon supernatural intervention to protect our children from oncoming cars, from cruelty on the playground, from harsh teachers. At each point of our children's growth, they leave us by degrees, and we must learn to give them again into God's hands.

But it's not just children we must learn to offer up. All the objects we hold dear require intentional sacrifice, and willing repetition seems a requirement in this walk toward obedience. I remember the night when, after years of struggle, after years of discipline and self-denial, I received the first copies of my first book. I heard that divine voice whispering to me,

"Can you give to me your Isaac? Can you give to me your writing?"

In shock, I responded (like Abraham, lifting my eyes to that place afar off), "Lord, You wouldn't ask me not to write, would You?"

The question came, adamant again without equivocation or pandering explanations: "Can you give to me your Isaac?"

I sighed. Of course I would offer up this thing I loved. I prepared the ass and stacked the wood and went plodding with a heavy heart to that far mountain. Fortunately, my writing was not required of me, just the existential intent of sacrifice, an important distinction to God. I have written and written since that dark encounter with the Lord.

THE SACRIFICIAL PRAYER

I have had to sacrifice so many Isaacs of so many kinds. My heart is a clutching heart, an owning heart, a proprietor's heart. I have had to offer up my love for my husband, my pride in a new home, my sense of satisfaction in the ability to earn my financial keep in the family, my fixation with a current creative project. There are people I love too much, positions that threaten my single-eyed devotion, cherished affections that dim the memory of that ancient proclamation: "Hear, O Israel: the LORD our God, the LORD is one. Love the LORD your God with all your heart and with all your soul and with all your strength. Do not follow other gods, the gods of the peoples around you" (Deuteronomy 6:4-5,14).

Why is this sacrificial prayer so important?

Because we humans are always in danger: The people we love, the possessions we love, the professions we love threaten to supplant the place God reserves for Himself in our soul. He desires our whole heart. But at our very essence we are idolatrous. We need to learn to offer up the Isaacs of our lives in the same way the gifts were given to us—with love, with love. Imagine God's delight when He watched Abraham actually place the kindling and wood on the pile of stones, when the old man sharpened his knife and turned toward his son. Finally! At last! Here was one man intent on following God.

Abraham's unnatural intents eventually were thwarted by the divine provision of a substitute ram, thicket-trapped, for the sacrifice. Reading the account, one can almost hear God sing, "I will surely bless you and make your descendants as numerous as the stars in the sky and as the sand on the seashore....And through your offspring all nations on earth will be blessed, because you have obeyed me" (Genesis 22:17-18). God always requires the intentional sacrifice of anything cherished, of any of the children of my creative womb—the work of my hands, the labor of my heart, the sweat of my soul. I am learning to sacrifice them before He asks, to gather the wood, to go to the mountain.

Do you have an Isaac you should offer today? Is there something too dear, too precious, that holds a grip on your heart? You'll never know a blessing compared to the one that takes place when God receives your sacrifice. Prepare the wood. Saddle the ass. Turn your eyes to that far-off land. Begin the lifelong pilgrimage. Offer up what you love in the same way it was given to you—with love.

Thirty-eight

GETTING GOD INTO FOCUS

MARTHA THATCHER

he photographer creates art when he is fascinated not by his camera, but by what he wants to bring into focus.

In the same way, the Christian who wants to live obediently must focus on God at all times. This is the primary characteristic of obedience: eyes on God. The author of Hebrews likens the Christian life to a race. He summons us to "fix our eyes on Jesus" as we run (Hebrews 12:2). After all, who else is the race for?

In Deuteronomy, multiple chapters record the nature and content of obedience. Blessings, curses, possibilities, and promises abound. A thoughtful reader is struck by the care God took to ensure that His people understood what He meant when He said He wanted them to obey. Then, in chapter 30, verses 19 and 20, the writer summarized, bringing the importance of obedience to a head: "This day I call heaven and earth as witnesses against you that I have set before you life and death, blessings and curses. Now choose life, so that you and your children may live and that you may love the LORD your God, listen to his voice, and hold fast to him. For the LORD is your life, and He will give you many years in the land he swore to give to your fathers, Abraham, Isaac, and Jacob."

Think back to Abraham. How could he raise the knife to kill Isaac, his son of promise? Was his obedience blind? No. Abraham focused on who God is—a God of the miraculous—and knew that God would keep His promise to bless the earth through his offspring, even if it meant raising Isaac from the dead. God's character provided Abraham's hope.

God's character provides our hope. We may not feel that we are in control of our situation, but God is in control. That is hope. We may not have energy and ability enough to carry out our responsibilities, but God is all-powerful and fully able to enable us step by step. That is hope. We may be shocked and reeling from an overwhelming storm, but God is the unmoving Rock beneath us, ready to be our help and refuge in the midst of our storm. That is hope.

The depth of who God is and the breadth of all He has done form the limits for our focus and the basis for our hope. Looking at Him and becoming aware of His character as related to our situation, we will find that our needs fall into perspective.

My camera has a focusing ring that allows me to choose what image will be central in the photograph. It didn't take me long to realize that if I draw one image into focus, I automatically put several others out of focus. Although there are ways to increase the focusing range, I rather like having a good part of the picture slightly fuzzy; it encourages singular attention. The crisp central focus leaves no doubt about what is important to me in the picture. The result is perspective.

God reveals Himself in the Bible. He tells us to "seek my face" (2 Chronicles 7:14). As we look to Him, we can answer with David, "Your face, LORD, I will seek" (Psalm 27:8). The focus of the loving and obedient heart is the God who first loved us.

I am talking about our chosen response to God. Whenever we zero in on our response to Him, there exists the subtle danger of "formulizing" the Christian life. And any time we think we have hold of a workable formula, we want to revert our trust and attention to the formula, losing our focus on God. In this way, we end up trusting in praise rather than in God or believing that prayer, rather than God, changes things.

Obedience is not a formula; rather, it is the attitude of a person who looks at God and says, "I want to follow You. I will do as You say, because I love You and want above all else to please You." With this heart attitude we bring every effort to bear on applying the Scriptures to the walk and talk of our days. That is a focus on God.

Thirty-nine

THE GREAT WAIT

RUTHANN RIDLEY

*Y*ale graduate Donald MacGavran got up at dawn, ate a light breakfast, fixed his bicycle, and began his daily rounds. He pedaled several miles to the nearest village, wound his way through the pitiful market, and parked his bicycle in front of a dirty hut. Although they could offer him no refreshment, the young mother and father were glad he had come. They told him about their current landlord problems and discussed the famine. He stayed for a while, played with the baby, and tried to encourage them. Then he pedaled to another hut on the opposite side of town. He visited several villages that day and hurried home before dark to avoid robbers.

He had been a missionary in India for almost thirty years, and not much had happened, at least not from his point of view. His dream had been to see masses of people come to Christ all over the world. When he was a mission secretary, his superiors became annoyed with his extreme emphasis on evangelism. So they demoted him to the position of back-woods evangelist.

MacGavran could have been discouraged. He could have become angry and bitter about the delay. Instead he persevered with the work he could do. Those years of patient endurance gave birth to the ideas that became his first book on church growth. Many more years of resistance to his call for evangelism in missions followed. Yet eventually his ideas took hold, and today few have influenced world evangelism as much as Donald MacGavran. God knew what kind of experience His man needed to accomplish his dream.

When we have done all we can, we must still wait for God to accomplish His purposes. As we wait, we can fix our eyes on Jesus as a companion who empathizes with our suffering and a Savior who is working behind the scenes. Difficult circumstances seem to increase our ability to experience intimacy with Christ. We reach out to Him more frequently and listen to Him more closely. Paul said he was willing to give up everything for this precious "fellowship of suffering." Jesus said, "Even the very hairs of your head are all numbered. So don't be afraid" (Matthew 10:30-31). He is intimate with our every loss, uncertainty, fear, and longing.

Jesus sits with me when my waiting is dark with enduring; when I wrestle with "what-ifs"; when my thoughts turn to recurring sin in my life; when I begin to fear that God won't answer my prayer because of that sin. He understands when I am afraid that a particular dream is too important to me; when I ask myself, "Can I trust God to love me and act on my behalf in this situation?" Yet the Bible says, "In all [our] distress he too [is] distressed" (Isaiah 63:9). He groans with us, but He also rejoices over us as we cling to Him alone.

Our Lord seldom leaves us with no evidence of His presence, no assurance of His power to bring the ultimate victory. A mother who had been praying for her daughters' spiritual commitment shared that when they seemed to be rebelling against God, there were always "flowers" along the way to show her that God was at work. One daughter would ask her to pray for something. Another would show an interest in her mother's Bible-study preparation. Both of them might surprise her with Scripture on a birthday card. The mother learned to focus on these positives.

THE GOD OF SURPRISES

God is a God of surprises. He makes walls fall down, creates miracle children, and causes water to gush forth from rocks. The phone rings, and the friend you've been longing to see says she's in town and wants to spend the weekend. Just when you've begun to focus your thinking on something else, God accomplishes your heart's desire.

His ways are higher than ours, and all His works are done in love. Hymn writer George Matheson says that when God asks His children to wait or leads them along a winding path, it is often because "He intends to perform a work that will bring them rich spiritual blessing."

It takes yieldedness to live in the now rather than to live singularly for something that will happen in the future: to say, "Thank You, Lord, for the simplicity of today: no ecstasies, no breakthroughs, no letters; just some time to rest, read, think, and laugh with the kids. It is good!"

Faith rests in the "rightness" of today. It endures and perseveres now. Hope, on the other hand, looks forward to future deliverance. It anchors itself in the sure promises of God.

Biblical hope is not a shaky effort to believe your desires will be fulfilled. It is not an "I wonder if" or "I hope I will" type of mentality. Scriptural hope is like an anchor or a fortress. It makes a person secure.

"Against all hope, Abraham in hope believed...being fully persuaded that God had power to do what he had promised" (Romans 4:18,21).

The majority of Scriptures that mention hope point to a specific future event or reward. Abraham's hope was that he would become the father of many nations. Peter spoke of the hope of an inheritance. David sang about the hope of God's help and deliverance. Our blessed hope is "the glorious appearing of our great God and Savior, Jesus Christ" (Titus 2:13).

Without hope, the wait for deliverance or vindication or healing or change or peace or joy or success or fulfillment would be impossible to endure. "But if we hope for what we do not yet have, we wait for it patiently" (Romans 8:25).

OUR FUTURE GOOD

Biblical hope is the assurance of a specific reward in the future. The word for "hope" in the original language of the Scriptures can be translated as a "happy anticipation of future good." We cannot leave the subject of hope, however, without addressing the one question we all ask: "Just how specific can my hope be? Can I decide what I want God to do for me, pray for it, believe, control my thoughts—never allowing a hint of doubt to creep in—and then be sure He will answer my prayer?"

There was a time when I thought that this approach might be valid. So after I finished writing my first book, I sent it to an interested publisher and prayed that God would cause that publisher to accept it. Often I said to the Lord, "You have to do this, because I'm believing You will." I thanked Him that He was in the process of achieving my desire even as I prayed, and I told others about my confidence.

I was treating God like reams of tissue paper, trying to force Him into

147

a small gift box labeled, "Book Published Now." I didn't realize how great the strain was until the day I discovered God had not answered my prayer. Suddenly He was sovereign again. He was no longer in a box. He was everywhere—immense, unmeasured, sufficient—fulfilling His own purposes, not mine. Realizing that the fruitfulness of my work did not depend on how hard I believed, but on God's power and wisdom, set me free.

We think we know how to design and interpret our own lives. But we are like precocious students of a master piano teacher. We labor over the notes of the piece He has given us until we are sure it can be no better. And we present it to Him, expecting Him to say, "Yes, this is the way your life should be. Your plan is perfect. I will support every note." Instead, He simply nods at our presentation and sits down to play the piece Himself. And we hear new worlds: variety, shape, depth, rich emotion, intricate skill. When He is finished playing we cannot speak. His artistry is profound. His interpretation is perfect.

"Your plan for your life is good," says the Lord, "but mine is better. It will exceed your highest expectations." If, at the end of a wait, we discover God has not given us what we have prayed for, we can be sure He will give us something better.

Who can say what the results of our willingness to wait in faith and persevere in hope will be? I cannot tell you specifically what God has in mind for you, but "your labor in the Lord is not in vain" (1 Corinthians 15:58).

Forty

SEEKING GOD THROUGH SACRIFICE

JONI EARECKSON TADA

We are to offer our bodies "as living sacrifices, holy and pleasing to God—this is your spiritual act of worship" (Romans 12:1).

A living sacrifice. I used to think of a bloody oblation on top of a brazen altar. Yuck. Well, that Old Testament image may not be all that different from what Paul meant in Romans 12. Frankly, when I read that verse I see myself on an altar. But this is where it changes—as soon as God strikes the match to light the flame of some fiery trial in my life, I imagine myself doing what any living sacrifice might do: I crawl off the altar!

This, to put it simply, is the dilemma Christians face. Living offerings have a way of creeping off the altar when the flames of a frustrating ordeal get a bit too hot. But the theme resounds through Scripture: He who loses his life for Christ's sake shall find it. Take up your cross—your altar of sacrifice—and follow Jesus. Since we died with Christ, we shall live with Him. If we die with Him, we shall reign with Him.

As demanding as it may seem, God says that we are to present our bodies as living sacrifices, for this is our *reasonable* service. What's more, while we're on the altar, we're to praise God for the trial, because He is using it to mold us into the image of His Son. As our bodies are living sacrifices, our lips offer the sacrifice of praise. Sound reasonable?

Humanly speaking, no. With God's grace, yes.

There's no getting around it. In view of God's mercies, in view of His single and great oblation for us, He asks for the only kind of spiritual worship that is holy and pleasing to Him. A living offering. Yes, you may squirm under the heat of the trial, but that doesn't change God's command. He's urging you today to get back up on the altar.

Believing and Living by Faith

A simple, childlike faith in a Divine Friend solves all

the problems that come to us by land or sea.

— HELEN KELLER

Forty-one

God's Definition of Faith

EDITH SCHAEFFER

*I*s there some magic formula to be discovered for manufacturing "faith?" Is there a way to unlock a supply cupboard containing the faith some people seem to have discovered? Is there a mysterious level only the properly initiated can reach, where faith is then freely given? Is there a beginning place for exercising faith, as one would the muscles of the leg, when one is a Christian? Upon whom can we depend [to explain our] lack of faith to carry out the literal admonition to "ask" rather than to "ask not?"

God speaks to us clearly concerning the basis for faith, and the primary exercise for our faith. "So then faith cometh by hearing, and hearing by the word of God" (Romans 10:17, KJV). Hearing has to do with physical ears, first of all—but with the mind simultaneously. Hearing is accompanied by some sort of action in our minds, if words in a language we understand are being used. It is the Word of God, which is truth being unfolded [via] a succession of meaningful words in human language.

The Word of God is the Bible. What makes it different is that it is what God has revealed to man, and is therefore true truth. What makes it different is not a floating, mystical, spiritual kind of "feeling," which bypasses language as it is normally used. Language can be used to say things that are not true, to deceive, to stir up responses that are wrong, to twist people's thinking. But when God's Word is spoken of, the basic difference is one of pointing out that there is a trustworthy, perfectly just, and holy Person verbalizing something that can be depended upon.

We are to listen to God's definition of "faith" with careful expectation of discovering what we have overlooked before, of really learning something that is true. However, it is to be learned with the same equipment with which God has created us to learn arithmetic, spelling, or how to bake a cake, plant a garden, or build a house that will withstand the storms. Understanding does not come immediately and completely in the learning process in most areas of life. Understanding usually takes some amount of time, but the first requirement of understanding, as parents often stress to their children, is hearing—listening and paying attention to the content of what is being said.

God tells us in Hebrews 11:3: "Through faith we understand that the worlds were framed by the word of God, so that things which are seen were not made of things which do appear" (KJV). What a staggering statement of fact, as well as a definition of what we are to start with in our exercise of faith. We are forcibly thrust back to the beginning of the Bible: "In the beginning God created the heavens and the earth" (Genesis 1:1), and we are told to believe that the living God has spoken the truth when He has said He created the heavens and the earth. We are to read with eagerness the Genesis account, thrilling at the opportunity to have faith, to begin at the starting place God has given, and to state in the most emphatic way we can: "I have faith to believe You, Creator God, that You have made what I see, taste, smell, and hear. I believe what you have verbalized in Your Word. I believe in Your creation of the universe. Thank You."

It is the God of the Creation in whom we are to have faith. It is His spoken Word we are to believe when He tells us He created the universe. Our faith that the Creation actually took place is to be our exercise of faith, as a foundation to having the faith [that enables us to] "ask." As we come with our requests "with thanksgiving" and thank God for what He has done in the past, we are to include thanksgiving for the act of Creation. "Let them praise the name of the Lord: for he commanded, and they were created" (Psalm 148:5, KJV).

Let us cast ourselves on our faces in the midst of the twentieth-century discussion and cry out for a reality of that faith to be such as will be pleasing to God. He has clearly given us the starting place. It is His definition of faith.

Forty-two

THE LAW OF FAITH

HANNAH WHITALL SMITH

J esus said unto him, 'If thou canst believe, all things are possible to him that believeth'" (Mark 9:23, KJV).

We know that all things are possible to God, and here our Lord tells us that all things are possible to us also, if we only believe. No assertion could be more distinct or unmistakable. The great thing for us, therefore, is to discover the law by which faith works, that we may know how to exercise this tremendous spiritual force declared by our Lord to be our birthright as children of God and partakers of His nature.

There are two Scripture illustrations that make it very plain what faith really is.

Through faith we understand that the worlds were framed by the word of God, so that things which are seen were not made of things which do appear. (Hebrews 11:3)

(As it is written, I have made thee a father of many nations,) before him whom he believed, even God, who quickeneth the dead, and calleth those things which be not as though they were. Who against hope believed in hope, that he might become the father of many nations, according to that which was spoken, "So shall thy seed be." And being not weak in faith, he considered not his own body now dead, when he was about an hundred years old, neither yet the deadness of Sara's womb: He staggered not at the promise of God through unbelief; but was strong in faith, giving glory to God; And being fully persuaded that, what he had promised, he was able also to perform. And therefore it was imputed to him for righteousness. (Romans 4:17-22, KJV)

The passage in Hebrews simply means that we know the worlds were framed by the word of God, because God says they were; we believe Him, without requiring any other proof but His Word. We were not there to see them so made, and we do not know anybody who was; but God says it, and we believe Him, and this is faith.

The passage in Romans is similar, only it illustrates faith in regard to a future thing instead of a past thing. Abraham is the Scripture pattern of faith, continually pointed to as such all through the Bible. Now what did Abraham do? He simply believed God, when He told him He was going to give him a son. He had no outward proof of it and no rational human hope, but he "against hope believed in hope" because God had said it, and he chose to believe God. Therefore, it is said of him that Abraham believed God, and it was counted unto him for righteousness.

The law of faith appears, therefore, to consist simply in two things: namely, a conviction of God's will, and a perfect confidence that His will must necessarily be accomplished. There are two passages that seem to me to set forth very clearly and definitely the working of this law.

> And this is the confidence that we have in him, that, if we ask any thing according to his will, he heareth us: And if we know that he hear us, whatsoever we ask, we know that we have the petitions that we desired of him. (1 John 5:14-15, KJV)

> And Jesus answering saith unto them, "Have faith in God. For verily I say unto you, That whosoever shall say unto this mountain, 'Be thou removed, and be thou cast into the sea'; and shall not doubt in his heart, but shall believe that those things which he saith shall come to pass; he shall have whatsoever he saith. Therefore I say unto you, What things soever ye desire, when ye pray, believe that ye receive them, and ye shall have them. (Mark 11:22-24, KJV)

Notice the process of faith—or in other words, the law of faith—as set forth in these passages. We are commanded to have the same sort of faith that God has (Mark 11:22). Now God's faith that what He desires will be accomplished, is of course absolute and unwavering. He knows it. And we are to know it also. Then we are to say so.

One passage says "ask," and the other says "say." I believe they are interchangeable words in this connection and that the prayer of faith is really a command of faith also. God spoke and it was done; so are we also, who are begotten of Him, to speak, and it shall be done also. We are to have the same sort of faith that God has, according to our measure. Romans 4:17 describes the sort of faith God has: "God, who quickeneth the dead, and calleth those things which be not as though they were" (KJV).

How much of this creative power of faith we His children share I am not prepared to say, but that we are called to share far more of it than we have ever yet laid hold of, I feel very sure. There are, I am convinced, many "mountains" in our lives and experiences, which might be overcome had we only the courage of faith to say to them, "Be thou removed," accompanied with a calm assurance that they must surely go. The difficulty is that we neither "say" the word of faith nor "pray" the prayer of faith. We say generally the word of doubt and pray the prayer of experiment, and then we wonder why our faith and our prayers are so ineffectual.

The old worthies surely must have understood the law of faith and known how to apply it, far better than we of the present day do. To them this "law" was a law that applied not only to their religion but to their life. They brought it into use not only on fast days or feast days but on ordinary weekdays as well. They applied it to every emergency. We of the present day make the mistake of limiting the working of this law to what we call the religious part of our lives. And yet it is evident that the Bible, in teaching us to "live by faith," must mean our daily living.

Let us make up our minds, then, to live by the "law of faith." Let us bring it to bear on our household affairs, on our business enterprises, on our social duties, and all and everything, in short, that concerns us, whether it be inward or outward, and see whether we, too, may not "obtain a good report through faith," and may triumph, as these old worthies did, over every emergency and every need of our lives.

Forty-three

PASSAGES OF FAITH

PAULA RINEHART

For the first time in my life I was up against a situation over which I had no control. No amount of effort could change the outcome. No seminar or book could help. Even the doctors, those white-coated wonders, just shook their heads and said, "I'm sorry Mrs. Rinehart, these things just take their own course. There's not much we can do."

Perhaps my feeling of uncertainty was magnified by the days I lay in bed, waiting to see if I could keep this small life growing inside of me. Maybe I just had too much time to think. But when I eventually miscarried, I felt as if I had lost more than a baby. The awareness that my life was turning out much differently than I'd ever imagined thrust me outside the protective bubble I'd been living in for years.

That small death was the first of a series of stinging losses in my mid-thirties. Within a few months I confronted a major family crisis. In addition, we found that our son had significant learning disabilities, and the book I was writing bit the dust. Like so many people in their thirties, I had discovered that I was not in control. That clear-eyed awakening was frightening. Almost nothing in my life seemed sure and certain anymore. Inside I was a bundle of questions and doubts. I, who had begun this spiritual journey on the trumpet call "God loves you and has a wonderful plan for your life," began to edge toward skepticism.

Somewhere during this time I picked up Gail Sheehy's book *Passages,* which explores the stages of adult development. I found myself intrigued with the idea that being an adult wasn't a matter of climbing some steep hill and then sitting on the top waiting passively for the end. Each "passage" of adulthood is marked by particular crises or turning points that hold potential for new growth. *Could it be,* I wondered, *that growing up spiritually is patterned in passages or phases too?* Maybe I had come to a critical juncture and didn't know it. Maybe real spiritual growth was more like a story of a pilgrim on his way home. If so, periods of doubt and disappointment were part of that process.

I began to see the lives of New Testament men and women in a new light. For the first time they seemed like real people. In their stories lay the outline of a basic cycle of spiritual passages that moved in ever deepening spirals from illusion to disappointment to real hope. As I found my story among theirs, I dared to wonder if my own disillusionment would dissolve into a different and deeper trust than I had ever known. But first I needed to look back at the beginning of my faith journey.

A FAITH THAT INSISTS

If you asked me for a word to describe the most rudimentary form of faith, I would choose "predictability." Early faith hopes against hope that God will move in our lives in predictable ways. We seem to think God's promises are connected by an invisible string to the dreams and expectations in our own minds. "If I do this, then God will…"

Faith, at this point, is a manageable belief system in which our faithfulness or obedience obligates God to bring about our desires. At its heart, it's a faith that insists.

The disciples started out with this kind of faith. Jesus told them over and over that He must suffer and die, and if they followed Him they would encounter their own measure of the same. But Christ's words fell outside the boundaries of the disciples' expectations and understanding. When Jesus was crucified, the disciples were stunned.

I believe this demand for certainty, for predictability, is where faith starts for all of us. I've spent the bulk of my life as a Christian in this passage of "predictable faith." Although faith of this sort may suffice for a time, it cannot bear the full weight of life. It is a subtle form of trying to conform God to our own image of Him.

God does not allow us to continue to reduce Him to a size and shape we can manage. He moves in our lives in ways that burst our categories and overwhelm our finiteness. Ironically, the crisis of disillusionment is what shakes our preconceived notions and beckons us to deeper faith.

THE DEPTHS OF DISILLUSIONMENT

The disappointment that leads to this second passage of faith is usually quite unexpected. To think that faith would turn to disappointment appears contradictory, as though God were defeating His own purposes. Yet we rarely see the extent of our expectations until, for one reason or another, they are not fulfilled.

At this point, many reactions are possible. Confusion and doubt are two of the most common ones. As John the Baptist sat in prison toward the end of his life—his disciples disbanded and his future uncertain—he felt the need to send a friend to question Jesus. "Are you truly the Christ, the One we've been waiting for?" Christ assured him that He was. And He did not rebuke him for needing that reassurance.

For some, disillusionment leads to cynicism and apathy, a kind of dead-in-the-road state, as though someone has let the air out of your tires. But it doesn't have to be that way. What feels like the end of faith actually holds the potential for its true beginning. When we let go of our determination to make God conform in safe, predictable ways, it is possible to receive something better in its place.

One of disappointment's hidden benefits is that it moves you out of your head—your cognitive understanding—into some of the messy, broken places in your heart.

I remember one summer when I felt defeated. The Bible became like a dead book to me. I went for weeks with almost no thought of prayer. And then one morning I woke up and the first thought that came to my mind was, *Paula, you're an angry woman.*

The moment I admitted the truth, a strange thing happened. I sensed God almost asking my permission, as it were, to be invited into the muck and mire of my struggle. Would I let Him lead me into some of the sealed-off compartments of my heart? Not the polished, presentable places, but the rooms where unacknowledged grief and fear and bitterness had been incubating for years? There were parts of me, He seemed to insist, that had yet to hear the gospel.

I was amazed to think that God would not turn away from me when I didn't even want to be with myself, when I was so inclined to turn my back on Him. I had not realized—on a deeper, more emotional level—that He cared that much.

In my early Christian life I saw faith as a set of propositions to be defended, a body of knowledge to learn and pass on, a storehouse of sure answers. But the faith that emerges out of broken dreams is different and harder to describe. There is room for mystery—for not knowing all the answers. The passage of faith that follows disillusionment begins when there is no experiential reason to believe. It is born in the fearlessness that comes when you've already lost a good portion of what you were so afraid of losing in the first place.

Somehow, you know God is there in the midst of this passage—in ways you didn't expect. He makes His presence known by the pain of His seeming absence. He doesn't necessarily change the circumstances; He gives you the courage to face and move through them.

Faith that withstands its own demise is free of the need to control life. It moves beyond the safe confines of predictability to a place where we begin to enjoy a relationship with a Person—a relationship that is often elliptical, full of ebb and flow, desert and garden. The focus of our faith shifts from discovering ways to get a fix on God to experiencing the reality that He is the One who has hold of us.

Forty-four

AUTHENTIC FAITH

CAROLE MAYHALL

*I*t's important to remember that our faith becomes authentic in everyday living, not just through some huge trial or mountaintop spiritual experience. In Colossians 3:17, the apostle Paul reminds us, "And whatever you do, whether in word or deed, do it all in the name of the Lord Jesus, giving thanks to God the Father through him."

That includes all things. When my husband left his associate pastor's position, we moved to California, where he ran a center for U.S. servicemen. My days were filled with scrubbing floors, making beds, and preparing meals for a crew of these men. It was there I realized a "good work" is anything you do in the name of the Lord. Everything I did, no matter how mundane, became a way to fulfill my calling as God's child. Approaching my role in life like this gave me a different perspective.

Ephesians 3:17-19 spells out the bottom line in making our faith authentic: "I pray that Christ will be more and more at home in your hearts, living within you as you trust in him. May your roots go down deep into the soil of God's marvelous love; and may you be able to feel and understand, as all God's children should, how long, how wide, how deep, and how high his love really is; and to experience this love for yourselves, though it is so great that you will never see the end of it or fully know or understand it. And so at last you will be filled up with God himself" (TLB).

According to the apostle Paul, our goal in life is to know God's love. The Living Bible translation of these verses uses the words *feel, understand,* and *experience* when it refers to this process. When we combine these actions with our personal acceptance of Christ, we can be confident that our faith is indeed real.

Forty-five

IN THE COMPANY OF DOUBT

VIRGINIA STEM OWENS

Consider Thomas, the patron saint of doubters. Originally attracted to Jesus and His invisible kingdom, Thomas perhaps feels cheated, tricked into believing what he can't see. When he loses his *raison d'être* after the crucifixion, he retreats to relying solely on his senses. The hearsay evidence of those who claim to see the risen Christ fails to convince him. He demands empirical evidence, almost boasting of his skepticism.

Thomas gets what he asks for. But not right away. He must stick around for a while before the evidence turns up. And during the later years that follow, when famine hits Jerusalem, when Romans burn the city to the ground, perhaps the old doubts return. It's hard for even the staunchest believer to sustain certainty in the face of adversity and delayed promises.

What sustains Thomas—what preserves us while we wander in the labyrinth of theological contradictions—is mercy. Not the supernatural mercy that propels us across spiritual crevasses, but the common mercy that God entrusts to physical nature. For whatever else we may be, our brains are indeed made of molecules. And on that lowly level they protect the life that animates them.

Our very taste buds and nerve endings serve as humble emissaries of this natural grace. Even when riddled with doubt, we can get hungry and eat or see an oncoming car and jump out of its way. On those days when we can't believe we're anything more than molecular arrangements, those intricate atoms keep us alive. They persist in their stunning complexity even while we insist on our own meaninglessness. When our minds can't hold on to faith, our bodies hold on to our brains.

We could do worse than follow the example of our physical bodies and their tenacious hold on life. Our bodies know what they want—life and health—and expend every resource fulfilling those desires. Perhaps if we focused our spirits' resources on our deepest longings, like a lens concentrating on sunlight, the intensity of desire would cauterize the doubt.

At one time or another, doubt overcame all the heroes of faith— Abraham, Moses, David, even Peter. Yet they survived their doubts, not because they worked out foolproof arguments for God's existence but because He remained the joy of their desiring. And their stories survived for us today as well. We still tell their stories, not because these believers eliminated doubt from their lives, not even because they stuck to the courage of their convictions, but because they clung tenaciously to their hearts' desire.

Forty-six

GETTING BEYOND SPIRITUAL DRYNESS

ELIZABETH SKOGLUND

D ry spells, feelings of spiritual deadness—these occur in the lives of all of us for a great variety of reasons. In the context of current Christian thinking, though, periods of feeling distant from God seem connected with sin and failure.

Most people I meet feel guilty when their feelings toward God are dead. This goes back to the "confess your depression" mentality. Certainly, sin does distance one from God, and the feeling of distance is, at times, a warning in each of our lives of something wrong. But what gets overlooked too often are the many other reasons for feelings of spiritual deadness.

PHYSICAL FACTORS

On the most simple level, spiritual dryness may arise from too little sleep, too much work, physical illness, poor nutrition, and lack of exercise. It is difficult to cultivate a sound spirit in an unsound body. Contrary to the thoughts of some, rest and general restoration of the physical body are vital to spiritual well-being. To burn out for God sounds highly spiritual, but I'm not at all convinced that this is usually God's plan for our lives. Perhaps for many of us the sin of spiritual dryness lies not in the feeling but in the exhausting high-wire living that brought us there. Then the depressive feelings are merely God-given signals of the need to refurbish our strength.

Yesterday I spoke with a lady who has dedicated her life to a continuous round of activities surrounding church life, children, husband, and other people's needs. Recently she has been feeling increasingly tired, irritable, and depressed. Her friends are critical of her moods and she feels very lonely. Then guilt sets in—guilt over such feelings and over her "weakness" for having to say no now and then.

Yesterday's conversation revolved around her plans for a desperately needed vacation at the beach, which she has almost destroyed already in her plans to center all activities around her three children and three of their friends. She can, and I hope will, have a week of rest combined with a happy time for her children. In the end they will benefit most from having a calmer, more pleasant mother. But in her guilt over being human and tired, the mother is almost unable to plan anything for herself.

The concept of distance from God and depressive feelings as they relate to physical weakness is backed up by numerous biblical examples. Elijah, who was a courageous prophet of God, came to the point where he sat alone in the wilderness after traveling all day and prayed to die. Lonely and exhausted, he gave up.

"I've had enough," he told the Lord. "Take away my life. I've got to die sometime, and it might as well be now." Then he lay down and slept underneath the broom bush.

Wisely, God did not argue with him, for He recognized the physical factors underlying the despair. But He sent an angel, who woke him up and commanded him to eat the bread and water he had brought to Elijah. Once again Elijah slept, and once again the angel woke him and forced him to eat. This time "the food gave him enough strength to travel forty days and forty nights to Mount Horeb, the mountain of God" (1 Kings 19:8, TLB). Then God spoke more to him and gave him instructions. But first God had recognized the priority of the physical in restoring Elijah to a place of service.

Similar stories can be told about men such as Jonah and Job. And in the New Testament, Christ often met physical needs of healing and hunger before He tried to relate to people on a spiritual level. Nor for Himself did He hesitate at times to go away from the crowds in order to regather His energies.

It is a lonely feeling to experience distance from God. Perhaps that is partly why men such as Elijah begged to die. But if we are merely exhausted, what a comparatively easy cure there is to such spiritual dryness. Yet how impossible that cure becomes if we spiritualize the physical and go on driving our already tired bodies!

OUR EMOTIONAL NEEDS

Sometimes the spiritual and emotional factors in our lives combine to bring a feeling of spiritual depression. A person who had experienced much disappointment and loss in past months said to me recently: "Sometimes I feel I have lost God, like He's remote or even angry at me." He feels guilt over such emotions, because they don't seem to be "what other Christians are experiencing." And in his guilt there is a deep loneliness, for distance from God and man is by definition a statement of loneliness.

Depression is an isolating feeling and thus feels distant from God. Anxiety causes feelings of having lost control, of being in danger, and this, too, can create feelings of having lost God. Guilt, even when misguided and unrealistic, creates deep feelings of God's disapproval. Yet in all of these emotions God *feels* gone. He is not really gone at all. In actuality it is perhaps at these times above all others that God truly desires to be close to us and help us. But too often we put more distance between ourselves and Him by thinking we have failed and our feelings of spiritual dryness mean God has left us.

Perhaps the crowning reassurance during periods of spiritual dryness is the knowledge that it is an experience common to those who walk most closely with God. Job, for example, was tested by loss of health, family, wealth, status, friends. No one understands, for it does seem as though Job has indeed come under God's displeasure. Yet in a deep agony of loneliness, seemingly abandoned by God and man, Job still trusts God in the unseen. Had Job not been so great, Satan would not have wanted to destroy him. And had Job not been so strong, God would not have allowed such a testing. For feelings of distance from God can be a great test of one's real faith in God. And it is a lonely test.

During such times, we are prone to ask what we have done that is wrong. It might be wise to add to that, "What is the level of my exhaustion at this time?" Or, "What have I done right that is being tested?" Or, "What am I about to do that is valuable to God?"

Finding Comfort in God

When tragedy and pain come our way, beloved,

the only place to hide and rest secure is in the

sovereignty of God.

— KAY ARTHUR

Forty-seven

UNDER HIS WINGS

JUDITH COUCHMAN

ast summer two birds took up housekeeping on my front porch, each in her own hanging pot of ivy. For several days I enjoyed watching them build nests, one twig at a time. But the situation changed when the birds became expectant mothers.

After the eggs arrived I couldn't step on the porch without both moms chirping with all their lung power. The cacophony grew so intense I began using the back door, except to greet visitors or check the mail box. Then after the babies hatched, the mother-noise was so annoying not even the cat would go near them. I stopped watering the plants in the hanging pots, preferring to purchase new foliage later than to bother the newborn birds.

The protective mama birds had successfully communicated their message: *Stay away from my children!* They took seriously their responsibility to guard and protect, to provide a safe haven until their young could fly.

It feels slightly odd to compare God to noisy birds, but Scripture speaks of the Lord's pinions, of hiding in the shadow of His wings. While escaping the clutches of King Saul, David the shepherd begged God, "Keep me as the apple of your eye; hide me in the shadow of your wings" (Psalm 17:8). David wanted God's eagle eye on him, the Lord's great wings hovering over him, for guidance and protection. He needed a safe place when, tired and afraid, he couldn't face the world.

I envision David singing in the black night:

Under His wings, I am safely abiding;
Though the night deepens and tempests are wild,
Still I can trust Him, I know He will keep me;
He has redeemed me and I am His child.

Likewise, when we pull away to refurbish the soul, we can imagine the Lord's pinions spread over us, His fierce love staving off intruders. But, unlike the fleeing David, we don't need to wait until danger lurks nearby. We can hide under God's wings at any time. In the mornings, during times of preparation for service, when we're in pain, when we're weary from the day, we can hide under His wings until once again it's our time to fly.

Under His wings, Under His wings,
Who from His love can sever?
Under His wings my soul shall abide,
Safely abide forever.

Forty-eight

A Hope Stronger
Than Our Hurts

HELEN GRACE LESCHEID

ow do you keep praying when you don't hear an answer? How do you cope when your problems won't go away…when your life seems to be on hold?

When my husband of twenty-eight years went through several years of severe depression, I asked myself these questions. When Bill signed himself into the psychiatric hospital on a warm September day, our family of seven was devastated. In fact, our whole community, who knew Bill as a strong Christian leader and well-loved high-school teacher, went into shock. Concerned and curious callers kept our phone ringing.

Once the shock wore off, though, messages of hope kept pouring in and I welcomed each one. But over the months, Bill's condition worsened. Despite all the treatment and the earnest prayers of faithful Christians on three continents, Bill's depression became so severe that he attempted suicide and threatened to kill his family. He was transferred from our local hospital to the university hospital, then to the locked ward of the state mental hospital.

Following a series of electric shock treatments, my husband improved enough to be discharged from the hospital. We were elated and deeply grateful. I told our friends, "God has answered your many prayers. Our nightmare has ended. Now we can forget the whole thing and get on with our lives."

Then, about two weeks later, Bill didn't want to get out of bed. With a sinking heart I watched the horrible downward spiral again. Bill was readmitted to the hospital. More electric treatments, more drugs with frightening side effects, more futile therapy sessions. Throughout the next several years the cycle repeated again and again. Then one day, Bill's psychiatrist leveled with me. "It could take another twenty years for your husband to get better," he said.

Raised and dashed hopes. Unanswered prayers. *How could I keep hoping when even the medical experts saw little reason to hope?* I wondered.

Many kind friends have reminded me of Scriptures that have given me hope, and I've written their names and the dates they encouraged me beside the verses. One verse in particular has become my prayer, and it is also the one that has the most names and dates recorded beside it in the margin. Romans 15:13 says, "May the God of hope fill you with all joy and peace as you trust in him, so that you may overflow with hope by the power of the Holy Spirit." Paul prayed this for the Roman Christians, who faced persecution and martyrdom. My friends have prayed it for me in my trials. As I've meditated on this short prayer I've found that biblical way to keep my hope alive. Perhaps what I have learned will encourage someone else to hope, even when it seems impossible to do so.

THE GOD OF HOPE

Through David's psalms I have discovered that a lasting hope is anchored not in circumstances but in the God of hope. Misunderstood by friends and family, hunted by King Saul, hiding in caves, and fearing for his life, David writes in Psalm 25, "I am lonely and afflicted. The troubles of my heart have multiplied...my enemies have increased and how fiercely they hate me!" (verses 16-19). Despite such discouraging circumstances David affirms, "No one whose hope is in you [Lord] will ever be put to shame" (verse 3). Why? Because "good and upright is the LORD...all the ways of the LORD are loving and faithful" (verses 8,10).

David didn't make the mistake so many of us make: We equate the goodness of God with the "rightness" of our circumstances. We're like the little girl who, when she got what she wanted, exclaimed, "God must really like me!" Or conversely, when things aren't going our way, we say, "Why is God punishing me like this?" But our circumstances are not an accurate reflection of God's goodness. Whether life is good or bad, God's goodness, rooted in His character, is the same. Knowing this, David could sing of the goodness of God whether he was peacefully tending his father's sheep or fearfully running from his enemies.

When by faith I affirm the fact that God is good and He is worthy of my trust, peace and joy return to my troubled spirit. It's all right not to understand. It's all right that my husband's latest treatment, which held forth so much hope, has failed. It's all right that in myself I don't have the resources to cope. God loves me and wants the best for me. As long as this is true, I'm secure. I shall cope.

A lasting hope is rooted in the God of hope, but it becomes mine only as I consciously choose to place my trust in Him. At one point the Old

Testament prophet Habakkuk was deeply troubled and he wrote:

> How long, O LORD, must I call for help,
>   but you do not listen?
> Or cry out to you, "Violence!"
>   but you do not save?
> Why do you make me look at injustice?
>   Why do you tolerate wrong?
> Destruction and violence are before me;
>   there is strife, and conflict abounds. (Habakkuk 1:2-3)

Yet, despite his circumstances, Habakkuk made this decision:

> Though the fig tree does not bud
>   and there are no grapes on the vines,
> though the olive crop fails
>   and the fields produce no food,
> though there are no sheep in the pen
>   and no cattle in the stalls,
> yet I will rejoice in the LORD,
>   I will be joyful in God my Savior. (3:17-18)

In a similar way, I've had to set the rudder of my will. *Where do I want to go with this experience?* I've asked myself. *Can I, like Habakkuk, trust God even when there's no visual evidence that He's at work?* Yes, since God is unchanging in His faithfulness to me.

But this resolve to trust God must be nourished daily. Nourishment comes to me privately as I feed on God's Word and pour out my heart to

Him. It comes to me corporately as friends stand with me and help restore my courage. I'm thankful that throughout the months and years I've found a network of supporters. Like Habakkuk I've discovered that "The Sovereign LORD is my strength; he makes my feet like the feet of a deer, he enables me to go on the heights" (3:19).

HE DOES NOT FAIL

In John Bunyan's book *Pilgrim's Progress*, Christian—on his way from the City of Destruction to the Celestial City—encounters many trials and interesting experiences. While visiting the house of the Interpreter, Christian sees a wall against which a fire blazes brightly. A man stands nearby throwing water onto the flames, yet the fire doesn't go out. To the contrary, the fire burns higher and hotter. As Christian watches he understands why: On the other side of the wall stands another man, who is pouring oil onto the flames.

This little story has often come to mind when one deluge of adversity after another has threatened to drown my hope. During these times I've felt so emotionally bankrupt that I've not been able to marshal my thoughts, let alone engage in positive action. All I've managed to do is lie on my bed and say something like this to the Lord: "I'm tired—totally spent. It hurts so bad I don't know what to do. But I trust You, Lord. You are kind and good. I depend on You." And in a mysterious way a quietness begins to seep into my troubled spirit. It's as though I'm in the presence of a great Counselor who's gently teaching me new ways to cope. There's a stirring in my heart and I can hear Him whisper, "Change will come. 'Not by might, nor by power, but by my Spirit'" (Zechariah 4:6). And I know that in time everything yields to God's will. Some Jerichos have to be walked around seven times, but the walls do eventually come down.

After four years in mental hospitals my husband rallied, to the surprise of everyone, and came home. When frequent panic attacks sent him to the hospital seven times in one year, each time Bill found the courage to come back out. In time, he worked at a maintenance job and began to teach Bible studies. But then, Bill readmitted himself to the mental hospital once again where he stayed for three and a half years. Eventually, he was discharged from the state mental hospital to a group home, where he is presently living with other individuals who, like him, cannot cope with life.

Feeling stripped of everything I hold dear—my husband, my marriage, our family home, and even my children for a time—my faith in a benevolent, sovereign God has steadily grown. Hope like strong inner cables has held me steady. The God of hope keeps pouring His oil onto the flame of hope and keeps it alive in me. He has not failed me so far, and I know He never will.

Forty-nine

THE GOD OF ALL COMFORT

HELEN CRAWFORD

he lump is cancerous," Dr. Gatchell said.

My first reaction was, "Lord, am I at fault? Have I done something? Are You punishing me?"

Through prayer, confession, and heart searching, God's Holy Spirit comforted me with the words of 1 John 3:21: "Dear friends, if our hearts do not condemn us, we have confidence before God." I now knew the air was clear—God was not condemning me.

Every spare minute I could manage before I went into the hospital I spent with my husband and daughter, reading the Word. I needed some special assurance, something personal to carry me through. I found it in Psalm 56:9: "Then my enemies will turn back when I call for help. By this I will know that God is for me."

A little phrase, "Even if he does not," kept coming to me the first day of my hospital stay. I later located it in Daniel 3 with the three Hebrew men in the fiery furnace. They said to King Nebuchadnezzar, "We do not need to defend ourselves before you in this matter. If we are thrown into the blazing furnace, the God we serve is able to save us from it, and he will rescue us from your hand, O king. But even if he does not, we want you to know, O king, that we will not serve your gods or worship the image of gold you have set up" (verses 16-18). I believed the Lord was requiring my complete trust in Him, whether or not I would be healed.

I don't recall now if it was the night after surgery or prior to it that I awakened in a cold sweat, totally overtaken by fear with the repetitious thought pounding like a jackhammer in my head: "I have cancer! I have cancer!" But in just a moment's time God's wonderful Spirit ministered these thoughts based on Proverbs 31:18: "Her lamp goes not out, but it burns on continually through the night [of trouble, privation, or sorrow, warning away fear, doubt, and distrust]" (AMP). My lamp of faith and dependence upon God need not go out, but full of the oil of His Spirit it can burn on. Immediate warmth, peace, and calm overtook the prior fear and cold. God was removing the robbers of fear, doubt, and distrust.

God was true to His promise in Isaiah 59:19: "So shall they fear the name of the LORD from the west, and his glory from the rising of the sun. When the enemy shall come in like a flood, the spirit of the LORD shall lift up a standard against him" (KJV). This "standard," or flag, was God's Word—totally adequate in the darkness of the night.

The ensuing year of chemotherapy was tiring, but now it is just a blur in my memory. My one prayer was to be able to raise my daughter, who was just entering high school. God not only answered that prayer, but He has given me additional years to enjoy our grandchildren. And I am still depending on the comfort and surety of God and His Word.

Peace in Spite of Distress

GIEN KARSSEN

I have told you these things, so that in me you may have peace. In this world you will have trouble. But take heart! I have overcome the world" (John 16:33).

Jesus did not leave His disciples with unrealistic expectations. "There is trouble coming for you," He said. "I warn you before it comes so that you will remember what I have said." Jesus' words were soon fulfilled. As the gospel spread quickly, people were converted and believed in Jesus Christ. This did not please Jesus' adversaries. They wanted to do away with the proclaimers of the gospel. James, the brother of John, was the first one killed by King Herod.

Peter was supposed to be the next victim. The night before his planned execution, he lay in a cell, chained between two soldiers and guarded by four squads of four soldiers each (Acts 12). The power of the Holy Spirit, earlier poured down from heaven, had changed Peter completely. The man who, because of fear for his life, had earlier denied his Lord three times, no longer was afraid. He was not concerned about what awaited him tomorrow. He was asleep! What better proof of inner peace is there?

Light shines brighter when the surrounding darkness is deeper. So inner peace manifests itself more clearly when outside circumstances are dark. Peace is also available to relieve the distress and misfortune none of us can escape, such as illness, adversity, unemployment, and misunderstanding. Each of us can experience peace in the midst of trouble over and over again.

Problems are bound to come. But God will be adequate for any and every situation. Jesus' victory over the spirit of this world will strip fear of its sting. Christ will give peace.

Fifty-one

THE GRACE OF SURRENDER

DEBRA EVANS

C ome to Me."

When the circumstances of life are beyond our ability to bear them, when there seems to be no way for things to work out, when the rapids hit and the boat threatens to capsize at any moment, when a sudden change in life plans cancels our dreams and reroutes the future, Jesus stands before us, and with His arms open wide, extends this incredible invitation. Surrendering our burdens at His feet and placing each heavy parcel before the cross, we can choose to close our ears to competing commands and confusing directions, and listen for God's voice alone.

Jesus said, "Come to me, all you who are weary and burdened, and I will give you rest. Take my yoke upon you and learn from me, for I am gentle and humble in heart, and you will find rest for your souls. For my yoke is easy and my burden is light" (Matthew 11:28-30). How could Mary have found her burden light on the way to Bethlehem, riding over bumpy roads on the back of a lumbering donkey? [Her story] prompts us to remember that God's graces appear in the midst of a consecrated life as it is actually lived, not in some far-off realm set apart from real human emotional experience.

Surrender never discounts or denies the reality of our suffering. When Jesus agonizingly prayed in the Garden of Gethsemane, "Father, if you are willing, take this cup from me; yet not my will, but yours be done" (Luke 22:42), there can be no doubt He knew what was at stake in the battle looming ahead. Quietly facing His accusers, He submitted to their authority, fully recognizing the costs involved. He understood what the terms of His surrender would be.

But that is not all: By laying down His life before His enemies in obedience to God's will, Jesus demolished the opposition.

Through surrender—bowing before God's mighty throne, laying each struggle before our Father in heaven, casting out all grief and heartache, giving up to Jesus every source of suffering and sin—we participate, with Christ, in His kingdom's victories. We cannot do it on our own. We are not supposed to even try to do it on our own. Heeding the Lord's command to surrender, we are continually surprised to find that, somehow, in a way that is totally beyond our comprehension, *He triumphs through us.*

Take heart, then. Pray for the grace of surrender. Receive all the peace and love Jesus freely offers. He is waiting. His arms are open. What He has done for the greatest saints, He surely can do for you and me.

Fifty-two

Enjoying God in Anguished Moments

J A N   J O H N S O N

When I entered the darkness of the church's auditorium, I wasn't sure why I had come. My kids were attending youth group several buildings away, and I felt drawn to sit there as I pondered my anguish over several friends at church. Thinking about one of them, a man with a terminal disease, I sat in his usual chair on the right side of the auditorium. There in the darkness I tried to pray for him, but words would not come. So I sat there and grieved for him. I found myself hunched over, elbows on my knees, head in my hands—just as he always sat. I knew I was praying for him, but I couldn't tell you what I said.

After a few minutes, I moved across the room to the seat where another friend usually sat. She felt betrayed by another church member and was crumbling inside, but she didn't want anyone to know it. I sat upright and tall in her chair, as she always did. She often wore a look on her face that said, "I'm going forth! Watch out!" and so did I as I sat in wordless prayer for her.

Finally, I moved toward the center aisle and slid into the seat of a friend who was separated from his wife. He always extended his arm across the empty chair next to him as if he were waiting for her to sit there, and I did the same. As I felt his grief, it became clear to me that each of them felt rejected by God in some way. My prayer found these words: "Help them know You love them."

After a while I left to run some errands, and when I returned to pick up my kids, I saw the lights on in the auditorium. I tiptoed in, and there sat one of the men I had prayed for, playing the piano. I hesitated, then walked toward him, leaned over, and said, "You are loved desperately by God." His face looked blank, but his eyes filled. "That's exactly what I need to hear," he said.

When anguish is too deep for words, it helps to sit in it as Job sat in the ashes (Job 2:8). This is contrary to the popular image of a Christian: a victorious overcomer who is always fine and never frustrated. Circumstances never puzzle these super-saints; people never bewilder them. For them, it seems as if God banishes pain and perplexity from life.

Scripture, of course, teaches otherwise. David writes, "The Lord is close to the brokenhearted and saves those who are crushed in spirit" (Psalm 34:18). And the apostle Paul was perplexed even as he did God's will: "We are hard pressed on every side, but not crushed; *perplexed*, but not in despair; persecuted, but not abandoned; struck down, but not destroyed" (2 Corinthians 4:8-9, emphasis added).

Times of anguish can transform us if we push away self-pity and put our energy into longing for God. In moments of brokenness, we can almost taste the psalmist's yearning:

As the deer pants for streams of water,
>   so my soul pants for you, O God.
My soul thirsts for God, for the living God.
>   When can I go and meet with God? (Psalm 42:1-2)

Those who see God as all sweetness and light are tempted to run from Him in painful moments. Instead, in our pain we are to cry out to God: "As a woman with child and about to give birth *writhes and cries out in her pain,* so were we in your presence, O LORD" (Isaiah 26:17, emphasis added).

In these distressing moments, we lay our brokenness before God. This advances us toward the goal of knowing Him because a broken spirit dissolves the wall of self-sufficiency that separates us from God. If we're to develop a familiar friendship with God, we cannot separate ourselves from Him during pain or temptation. The lifetime process of transformation involves God purging us of our tendency to push Him away and His wooing us into union with Him and His loving will for the world.

In the New Testament, it was the broken who came to know Jesus. Think of the woman who had hemorrhaged for twelve years, desperate, having spent all her money but finding no cure. Coming up behind Jesus, she quietly felt the edge of His cloak (Mark 5:25-34). Like her, we can use our brokenness to finally accept that our bag of tricks for living life is not nifty enough. No amount of self-help books will rescue us. No more "looking good, kid" facades—we freely admit our pain and temptation to God. Our failures strip us of our self-protection, making us vulnerable to God, just as the cured woman fell at Jesus' feet, trembled with fear, and told Him the "whole truth" before the crowd of people (Mark 5:33).

Perhaps you can accept that we can find closeness with God in times of irritation and anguish, but you wonder what they have to do with *enjoying* God's presence. Enjoyment comes from receiving pleasure, but it also comes from appreciating the benefits of deepening our intimacy. When we confess our shortcomings to God, we can enjoy His presence because we know that God's love envelops us in spite of our flaws. No one else so completely understands, loves, and challenges us. This familiar friendship doesn't take away the pain or temptation, but it gives us the strength to stand firm.

Asking and Receiving from God

Prayer is not eloquence, but earnestness;

not the definition of helplessness, but the feeling of it;

not figures of speech, but earnestness of soul.

— HANNAH MORE

Fifty-three

Our Need to Ask

Colleen Townsend Evans

any people—among them, many Christians —believe that petitionary prayer is selfish, and they frown upon it. "God is too great, too busy, to be involved with my little concerns," they say. Or if they don't admit it openly, they secretly believe it in their hearts, which keeps them from enjoying their full right as a child of God.

But it was Jesus who said, "Ask and it will be given to you; seek and you will find; knock and the door will be opened to you" (Matthew 7:7). He told us to ask our Father for our daily bread—and what could be more basic than that?

Prayer is the little child stretching its arms up to its father and pleading, "Up, Daddy! Up!" and repeated prayer is simply adding, "Please?" It is precisely because God is our Father—a loving Father who desires to give good things to His children—that He tells us to ask of Him. Jesus exclaimed, "Is there a father among you who will offer his son a snake when he asks for fish, or a scorpion when he asks for an egg? If you, then, bad as you are, know how to give your children what is good for them, how much more will the heavenly Father give the Holy Spirit [or a good gift] to those who ask Him!" (Luke 11:11-13, NEB).

We never have to make an appointment to talk to God, and we don't have to go through channels. We have immediate access to the Creator of the universe through our special relationship to Him. When you and I became children of God, by accepting the gift of life He offers through His Son, we were given family rights and responsibilities. We have the right to ask God to supply our needs as we seek His kingdom and His justice, and we have the responsibility to love Him and obey His commands.

All of prayer is a relationship with God, and "asking prayer" is a special part of that relationship. Often it is the first step in our relationship with God. For we are needy creatures, and often our needs reach crisis proportions. To whom, then, do we turn? As we tell God about our needs and listen to Him answer us—either by providing for our need or by using our need and openness to reveal something He wants us to see—our relationship with Him grows.

It is interesting to me that the words "ask, seek, knock" in Luke 11 are (in the original Greek) all in the present imperative, the tense of continuing action, so that the meaning is "continually ask," or "keep on seeking and knocking." It is not only acceptable to God that we ask; He wants us to ask—He earnestly desires that we ask—He requests and commands us to ask. For as we keep on asking, seeking, knocking, we keep our relationship with God alive, vital, and in the present.

The daily discipline of directing our specific requests to God allows us to build our relationship with Him. As we grow in faith, we will learn other ways to pray to God, such as simply praising Him for who He is, [offering] adoration and thanksgiving, or confessing where we have failed Him and His plan for the kingdom. In all these ways we will set our minds and hearts in tune with Him. But petition, or asking, is one of the closest, simplest, most basic kinds of prayer. It is God meeting us at the point of our need for Him, and this, after all, is what our daily bread represents. That is why God is pleased when we ask for it.

THE PERSISTENT FRIEND

Immediately after teaching the disciples to say, "Give us this day our daily bread," Jesus told a story:

> Suppose one of you has a friend who comes to him in the middle of the night and says, "My friend, lend me three loaves, for a friend of mine on a journey has turned up at my house, and I have nothing to offer him"; and he replies from inside, "Do not bother me. The door is shut for the night; my children and I have gone to bed; and I cannot get up and give you what you want." I tell you that even if he will not provide for him out of friendship, the very shamelessness of the request will make him get up and give him all he needs. And so I say to you, ask, and you will receive; seek, and you will find; knock, and the door will be opened. For everyone who asks receives, he who seeks finds, and to him who knocks, the door will be opened. (Luke 11:5-10, NEB)

It is important to realize not only that this man was granted his request by his friend because he asked in simple faith, believing his friend's ability and desire to help him—actually, he embarrassed his friend into helping him!—but also that this man had a good reason for needing the three loaves: another friend was asking him for them!

What resources do you need in order to live and to help others? An education, presentable clothing, a place to live, dependable transportation, materials for crafts, money, time, physical energy, a loving and joyful spirit? These are some of the "loaves" you may receive from your Father—if you ask for them. God not only has the desire to give us our daily bread, He has the ability to give it to us.

How easy it is for some of us (me!) to begin to depend on or trust ourselves—our efforts, our experience, our talents—and forget that God is the giver of all, and the only One worthy of our ultimate trust. Though it often hurts—even humiliates me—I am grateful every time God pulls me up short and reminds me of this basic truth of life in Christ. We must constantly remember our need for and our dependence upon our heavenly Father as the source of all life, physical and material as well as spiritual.

BEARING FRUIT FOR GOD

In John 15 we read, "Ask whatever you will, and it shall be done for you. By this my Father is glorified, that you bear much fruit" (verses 7-8, RSV). This tells us another important reason why we must ask God to supply our daily bread. Once we have accepted His Fatherhood, He has fruit for us to bear and work for us to do!

In Matthew 25 Jesus tells a story about three servants whose master entrusted each of them with different amounts of his gold and told them to invest it while he was away. When the master returned to take an accounting of the investments, he found that the first two servants had doubled his capital and brought him a handsome profit. The master called those two servants "good and trustworthy," and said to them, "You have proved trustworthy in a small way; I will now put you in charge of something big. Come and share your master's delight" (verses 21,23, NEB).

But the third servant, in fear, had simply hidden his master's gold in the ground. The story ends with the master's wrath at that servant, whose fear prevented him even from putting the money in a bank where it could have drawn interest.

By means of this story, Jesus was telling us that God is like that master. He has entrusted us, His servants, with some of His gold—in the form of time, energy, ability, money, experience, and tools—and He wants us to invest it wisely. If we are honestly trying to do the Lord's business, He will also supply whatever else we need to get the job done.

Asking God for what we need, then, is a vital link in the chain of prayer. We ask—and we ask again—and our persistence clarifies our desires. We ask, because in framing our specific daily requests, we are reminded of our dependence on our Creator as we open our hearts to Him, allowing Him to commune with us. We ask because the resources we need will enable each of us to do the work God, our Father, has assigned to us. And we ask because what we need is not only for ourselves, but for the glory of God and His kingdom, for the blessing of His world.

Fifty-four

THE BLESSINGS
AND BENEFITS OF PRAYER

BECKY TIRABASSI

*J*ust to pray without ceasing for one hour seemed like a monumental achievement in mastering a difficult spiritual discipline, but my deeper walk with Christ has truly been most meaningful to me. Yes, amazing answers to prayer elicit whoops and hollers, and persevering prayer teaches endurance, but spending time with Jesus—perhaps as His disciples did, laughing, crying, complaining, proposing, deliberating, submitting, confessing, and praising—has been the joyful part of our walk together.

Had people told me ten, even five years ago that I would be a prayer motivator, I would not have believed them, nor would my closest friends. I am often prejudged as never serious, perhaps even flighty, until I open my mouth. And of all the suitable topics someone of my personality profile could begin to expound upon, prayer would—without exception—be the last one picked by others as the love of my life.

Perhaps that paradox is the greatest argument I have in my defense when others offer their reasons (or excuses) for not praying. My experience in prayer proves the point that it is not race, sex, denomination, vocation, or education that singles out a person to be an effective pray-er. It is simply one's decision to spend time with the Lord. How one arrives at that decision—whether out of crisis, great need, humiliation, or persuasion— seems immaterial. It is a matter of one's time—priorities, personality, and profession all set aside and boiled down to one question: "Will I make time for God?"

When answered with a resounding, "Yes, no matter what the cost," then the inevitable results of a deeper walk with God occur *because of prayer*.

Prayer allows God's presence into all areas and aspects of one's life, beginning with simple daily decisions and culminating with one's life's purpose. The combination of prayer and the Word takes conjecture out of life and replaces it with certainties. And in the practice of prayer one is escorted farther and deeper into knowing and loving God.

Therefore, imagine one's surprise in stopping after five years of a long journey to look back over the mountains and valleys, to assess progress and be in awe of the unexpected benefits of prayer: The results of diligent prayer appear as illustrious jewels of immeasurable wealth, and just to read a list of them is appealing, but to experience them as personal possessions is life-changing!

On that journey of daily prayer and Bible reading I have experienced and benefited in six areas of personal spiritual growth, not because I am a woman in ministry, but because I am a person intent on spending time alone daily with God.

I discovered that:

- Prayer fuels faith to dream and hope and risk.
- Prayer "woos" us to the Word by our need to hear God's response to our requests.
- Prayer teaches trust in God through waiting upon His timing.
- Praying reveals God's plan and our purpose in opening up to us detailed directions for both the present and the future.
- Prayer releases God's power to live and walk in the super-natural realm of the Holy Spirit.
- Prayer unleashes love for God—emotional, real, and all consuming.

Who, then, having thought through the benefits of prayer, would consciously decide to eliminate, forget, or neglect time with God? Let's walk on...

Fifty-five

When You Don't Know How to Pray

JAN SILVIOUS

So how can you pray in a way that makes a difference?

Praying is similar to having wisdom—the whole direction must come from God. Effective prayer does not originate with you, nor is it something magic you can drum up by using just the "right" words. Romans 8:26-27 tells us, "In the same way, the Spirit helps us in our weakness. We do not know what we ought to pray for, but the Spirit himself intercedes for us with groans that words cannot express. And he who searches our hearts knows the mind of the Spirit, because the Spirit intercedes for the saints in accordance with God's will."

We are told that we don't know how to pray as we should. So when you pray for your situation, confess that right up front. Opening your dialogue with God with the simple sentence, "I don't know how to pray as I should," can roll a heavy burden off your shoulders. You don't have to think up what to pray or how to say it. You don't have to rummage through the right prayer book to find the perfect prayer. All you have to do is confess that you are totally clueless as to how to pray, and then God promises that the Spirit Himself will pray through you with groanings that cannot be uttered. To those who are related to Him, God promises help in their helplessness.

Fifty-six

SENDING TELEGRAPH PRAYERS

AMY CARMICHAEL

O ur Father loves us too much to let us pass through life without learning to endure. So I want you to welcome the difficult little things, the tiny pricks and ruffles that are sure to come almost every day. For they give you a chance to say no to yourself, and by doing so you will become strong not only to do but also to endure.

Whatever happens, don't be sorry for yourselves. You know how our Lord met the tempting "Pity Thyself" (Matthew 16:22, Authorized Version margin). After all, what is anything we have to bear in comparison with what our Lord bore for us?

I know that each of you is in need of continual help if you are continually to conquer. I have splendid words to give you; they are from the first verse of Psalm 46: "a very present help" (KJV).

Our loving Lord is not just present, but nearer than thought can imagine—so near that a whisper can reach Him. You know the story of the man who had a quick temper and had no time to go away and pray for help. His habit was to send up little telegraph prayers—"Thy sweetness, Lord!"—and sweetness came.

Do you need courage? "Thy courage, Lord!" Patience? "Thy patience, Lord!" Love? "Thy love, Lord!" A quiet mind? "Thy quietness, Lord!"

Shall we practice this swift and simple way of prayer more and more? If we do, our Very Present Help will not disappoint us. For Thou, Lord, hast never failed them that seek Thee.

Fifty-seven

Two-Way Communication with God

FLORENCE LITTAUER

onsider adapting these steps for use during your prayer time, making it a two-way communication with God.

• *Affection.* Many times, because of damage in our childhood, the hardest words for us to receive from the Lord are "I love you." Listen quietly. If the first words you hear are words of condemnation, write them down and then write across those words, "These words are a lie! Romans 8:1 states, 'There is therefore now no condemnation to them which are in Christ Jesus, who walk not after the flesh, but after the Spirit' (KJV)."

Keep listening until you hear that still, small voice whisper, "I love you!" Then write it down and thank Jesus for His everlasting love.

• *Reflection.* Often we get in the middle of a mess and we think, *How in the world will I ever get out of this?* In Deuteronomy 5:6 the Lord states, in essence, "Remember that you were slaves in Egypt and that the Lord your God brought you out of there with a mighty hand and an outstretched arm."

Take time to reflect on the Egypts God has brought you out of. Write them down. Thank God for rescuing you then, and thank Him for how He is going to rescue you this time. Write down the thoughts He gives you.

• *Correction.* First we need to examine ourselves to see if there is something we need to confess, someone we need to forgive, or someone we need to ask to forgive us. Also, this is a time when we can ask God if He wants to change our perspective on something. This could be a current situation or something that happened to us in our childhood. As God brings a memory to our minds, we can invite Him into the scene and ask Him to give us His perspective.

In your prayer time, write down what the Lord shows you. "Behold, thou desirest truth in the inward parts: and in the hidden part thou shalt make me to know wisdom" (Psalm 51:6, KJV).

• *Direction.* "I will instruct thee and teach thee in the way which thou shalt go: I will guide thee with mine eye" (Psalm 32:8, KJV). As we learn to ask the Lord specific questions, He will give us specific answers. "Your teachers will be hidden no more; with your own eyes you will see them. Whether you turn to the right or to the left, your ears will hear a voice behind you, saying, 'This is the way; walk in it'" (Isaiah 30:20-21).

• *Inspection.* We must always compare to Scripture what we hear. Scripture is the final and true authority for the Christian, so if what we hear contradicts Scripture, we should ignore it and hang on to the Scriptures. Job 12:11 states, "Does not the ear test words as the tongue tastes food?" It is also wise to consult with other Christians if there is any question about the validity of what we have heard. "Where no counsel is, the people fall: but in the multitude of counselors there is safety" (Proverbs 11:14, KJV).

Fifty-eight

INGREDIENTS FOR PRAYER

CORRIE TEN BOOM

*I*n the cell of a prison a woman lies on her cot with a bored expression on her face. She has a cheap novel in her hand, but it does not interest her much. Her needlework lies neglected on her chair. It is warm, and it is Sunday. Does she miss her daily work, which, although monotonous, helps her to get through the day?

I am visiting the cells after the sermon—an unusual privilege. Although I am allowed to speak at meetings in prisons, the follow-up work is usually left to the regular prison evangelists. I sit near the Dutch woman and for a short time can share her life in the small cell—colorless, monotonous, without any view. I know so well what it is like from my own experience. I feel such great love and compassion for this woman and pray that the Lord will give me entrance to her heart.

The ice is broken sooner than I expect, and we have a heart-to-heart talk. To begin with, the conversation is about baking cakes—a typical reaction engendered by the hunger that results from a monotonous diet. Carefully I try to turn our talk to deeper things. I discover that she has quite a good knowledge of the Bible, and it is easy to speak to her about the eternal truths. She knows that Jesus died for her on the cross, but she is a backslider.

"Do you sometimes make use of the time that you are alone to pray?" I ask.

"I don't know how to pray. Tell me something of your own prayer life."

I explain, "For cakes you need ingredients, and you need them for prayer, too. For instance, the ingredients of a prayer could be (1) the promises of God, (2) our problems and needs, (3) faith to bring these two together. If you don't understand me, I'll give you an example.

"Yesterday I was in darkness—really depressed. I didn't know what to do. When this happens I quietly spend a few minutes trying to find the reason. I can imagine a rich lady gathering her bills together once a week and writing out her checks. My Bible is my checkbook; my cares and problems are the bills. The devil tells me that the Bible is frozen capital, but he is a liar. All promises of God are in Jesus, yea and amen.

"I asked God to show me the reason for the darkness. God will give His children a clear answer when they are willing to listen in obedience. It is a question of making use of the quiet time. Then I wrote down the thoughts that came into my head. Finding the reason for the darkness is in itself a work of liberation. After making my list I took my Bible to 'pay my bills.'"

Then I continue, "The first thing I had written was that I was afraid for my health. Next week I must go to Japan, and I wondered if my body would stand the different climate—I am no longer young. I read Romans 8:11: 'Nevertheless, once the Spirit of him who raised Christ Jesus from the dead lives within you, he will, by the same Spirit, will bring to your whole being new strength and vitality' (Phillips). I said, 'Thank You, Lord. That is for me.' That 'thank You' meant that I had endorsed a check.

"The next thing on my list was that I was feeling downhearted. The church where I am speaking this week had organized a prayer meeting. I went to that meeting, but nobody else arrived. I had to pray alone. Then I read Romans 8:27, 'The Spirit prays for those who love God,' and verse 34, 'Christ prays for us' (Phillips). I understood then that there had been a prayer meeting, for if you are praying, the Lord is praying, and the Holy Spirit is praying, and that makes a prayer cell. I said, 'Thank You, Lord,' and another bill was paid.

"Thirdly, there followed my feeling of guilt. I had been tempted to gossip. No, it wasn't slandering. Everything said was true, but it was negative. Paul wrote in Romans 14, 'After all, who are you to criticize the servant of somebody else, especially when that somebody else is God? It is to his own master that he gives, or fails to give, satisfactory service. And don't doubt that satisfaction, for God is well able to transform men into servants who are satisfactory....Why then criticize your brother's actions?' (verses 4,10, Phillips).

"There were other sins I had committed for the umpteenth time: worry, selfishness, and so on. I read Romans 8:1: 'No condemnation now hangs over the head of those who are "in" Christ Jesus. For the new spiritual principle of life "in" Christ Jesus lifts me out of the old vicious circle of sin and death' (Phillips). I said, 'Thank You, Lord. The devil is strong, but You are Victor.'

"The last thing I had written down was that deep in my heart I was afraid to go to Japan. I do not know the language, nor what awaits me there. I wondered if people would help me, and if I should be able to find my way around. What a shame to have such doubts. The Lord has carried me through a most terrible time in prison. Won't He take care of me in Japan? I read the words of victory at the end of Romans 8: 'Who shall separate us from the love of Christ? In all these things we win an overwhelming victory through him who has proved his love for us' (verses 35,37, Phillips).

"My last bill was paid, the checks written. The darkness was all gone. I saw again that God's promises are greater realities than our problems. How exceedingly rich we are when we do not limit the promises of the Bible by our unbelief."

The woman says to me, "When you talk like this, I really long to live the Christian life again. I am going to do my best."

I look smilingly at her. "Do you see this stick? Do you think it is possible for it to stand upright on its own? Of course not, for it is not the nature of the stick to stand by itself. It can do so only when my hand keeps it steady. It is not the nature of human beings to be able to stand on their own. They can do it only when they surrender to the hand that will keep them from falling. Look, here in Jude 24 it is written: 'Now to him who is able to keep you from falling and to present you before his glory without fault and with unspeakable joy'" (Phillips).

For a moment we are quiet together, and I know that the Holy Spirit works in her heart. Then she surrenders to the Hand that was wounded to save her.

Fifty-nine

Praying God's Word

CHERI FULLER

hy pray Scripture? As I talk with women, one of their frustrations with prayer is knowing what to say to God or how to express it. "It sounds better to me when someone else prays," said one woman. "I don't feel my words are right."

Without His Word, I find our prayers become dry, lifeless, and vague. With His Word, our prayers are nourished and what we need to pray is illumined. God's words are alive and active, sharper than a two-edged sword, Hebrews 4:12 tells us. God promises that His Word will bear fruit: "So is my word that goes out from my mouth: It will not return to me empty, but will accomplish what I desire and achieve the purpose for which I sent it" (Isaiah 55:11).

My friend Melanie has seen how praying God's Word can fulfill His purpose. Several years ago she was deeply concerned about her sister Karen. She wasn't walking with Christ, and her two teenagers had run away from home in rebellion, refusing even to speak to their grandparents or

Melanie. Melanie knew other family members had tried to talk with Karen, but talking had no effect.

So Melanie set aside special pages in her prayer journal. On the left side, she wrote down what she was praying for: her sister's salvation, her niece's and nephew's return home and to Christ, the relationships. In the middle of the page, she wrote out verses she was going to pray for her sister. And on the right side of the page at the top she wrote, "Date Fulfilled."

Every day instead of moaning to God about the awful situation, Melanie prayed those verses. Even though she heard discouraging news about the niece and nephew, she kept praying God's Word. And as she did, God strengthened her faith that He was going to do the impossible.

Within a year, Karen was saved, and the relationship had been restored. The wayward teens had miles to go in maturity, but they were back on a positive track.

"The more we incorporate the Scriptures into our praying, the more likely we are to pray in the will of God, for God always stands behind what He has said," says Judson Cornwall. Psalm 138:2-3 confirm it: "For your promises are backed by all the honor of your name. When I pray, you answer me, and encourage me by giving me the strength I need" (TLB).

When we pray those promises, our prayers become filled with faith instead of doubt. We trust God to fulfill the promises in His way and on His timetable.

Enjoying the Personal Creator

When God finds a [person] that rests in Him and is

not easily moved, He gives the joy of His presence,

which entirely absorbs the soul.

— CATHERINE OF GENOA

THE JOY-FILLED CHRISTIAN

JILL BRISCOE

I have a missionary friend who labored for years in France, a difficult mission field because so few there have a real understanding of the gospel or any connection with the church. During her twenty-six years of service, my friend had led very few to the Lord.

As her extended furlough to the United States came closer, something happened to every one of those who had made professions of faith. One died. One moved away. The remaining one fell away from God. For her many years of hard work she was left with nothing to show for her efforts. She wondered what she would tell her home church.

Later my friend wrote me a letter. In it she said, "When I can't praise God for what He has allowed, I praise Him for who He is in what He has allowed." I was so struck by her words that I wrote them in my Bible. My friend, despite the fact that there was little joy in her circumstances, found joy in her God.

In the world's mind, joy is a feeling, a good giggle, a sense of happiness. It is an emotion that is contingent upon everything going well or a life with no problems. Christian joy, however, is different. It has nothing to do with whether our life goes as we want it to. My friend's experience in France perfectly illustrates this truth about Christian joy. I'm certain her heart was breaking as she saw those in whom she had invested her life fall away from the Lord. She could have easily looked back and said, "What a waste. I could have been doing something else."

Instead, she had joy, because she knew that in spite of her disappointment, God was at work in her life and she was doing what He wanted her to do. The joy we can expect as Christians is deeper than emotion. After all, the Holy Spirit doesn't come into our hearts to do His deepest work in the shallowest part of us.

THE ELEMENTS OF JOY

If Christian joy isn't a fleeting emotion or a smile, what is it? I've found it helpful to define joy by looking at two of its most vital elements.

First, joy is hope. The opposite of joy is despair. Despair is a dark place where there is no hope of life ever getting any better. Joy whispers, "There is hope!" If a despairing person can begin to hope or believe things can change for the better, then joy creeps in. Joy massages the tight neck muscles and relaxes you. Joy and hope are inseparable. We may not always experience joy. Sometimes, as the Scriptures say in Psalm 30:5, "Joy comes in the morning" after the long, dark night is over (NKJV). Many times when joy is not felt, it is possible that it's there all the time disguising itself as hope—a hope that leads to joy.

Second, joy is confidence. This confidence comes from knowing our God is a God of the future. He is in control of our tomorrows. Knowing He is in charge gives us an overwhelming sense of peace and security. To me, joy is a settled sense of well-being. Joy leads us to trust God. And yet this doesn't just happen to us. We need to cooperate. We need to tell God, "Though I am out of control I believe You are in control. Though my life and relationships are disintegrating, I believe You are complete and active though I cannot see You working."

Not long ago I was praying hard for a terrible situation. The more I prayed, the worse the situation became. What was God doing? I fretted. Why wasn't He busy answering all these earnest petitions?

We live by the side of a lovely lake and, rising early one morning, I went and sat by it. The surface was like a millpond—still and smooth until a fish jumped up here and there sending ripples across the surface. It was then I seemed to hear the Lord ask me, "Jill, do you have to see the fish jump to believe that it is here?" I wanted to say, "Yes, Lord!" but in reality I knew, and He knew, I didn't need to see the fish jump. I knew that underneath that glass-like, still surface the lake was teeming with activity. So I decided to have confidence in the Lord—to trust Him with my heartache and prayer and let Him answer them when He was ready. At that moment peace came and a measure of joy returned to my unhappy heart.

I believe God, through His Spirit, grants us love, joy, and peace no matter what is happening in our lives. As Christians, we shouldn't expect our joy to always feel like happiness, but instead recognize joy as an inner security—a safeness in our life with Christ.

As joy-filled Christians should we always wear a perpetual smile on our faces? No. As I've just said, at times life is tough and we don't feel cheerful. I've told women going through hard times, "You're not going to feel very good. I don't expect you to smile." The relief I see on the faces of women who are told they don't have to wear an artificial smile is amazing. Like these women I counsel, we, too, can take comfort in knowing we can be somber, serious, even burdened, yet still have joy.

JOY IN GOD'S WILL

Our joy as Christians is not based on circumstances but rather on being in God's will and doing what we were created to do. If we are living as God wants us to live, we will feel a sense of inner peace, and that is the joy we are promised as Christians.

Some of us stumble, however, in thinking joy from being in God's will should equal feelings of happiness. That isn't always the case, as my missionary friend articulated so well in her letter. Doing God's will doesn't guarantee you'll feel happy about the position you're in. In fact, you might very well be unhappy in a certain situation where God calls you to serve.

During one point in our ministry, my husband, Stuart, was on the road for long periods of time. There was absolutely no question in either of our minds that we were in the center of God's will. But I can tell you there were many lonely hours and days, even months, when God's will didn't feel like too much fun at all! And yet, I knew if Stuart stayed home, I'd feel a whole lot worse than if he were away! "How is that?" you may ask. Because you can't experience lasting joy if you deliberately turn away from God and what He has given you to do. To be holy rather than happy then becomes your choice. And the choice to be holy brings joy.

The pursuit of holiness won't always be a happy venture. If you doubt that, just read any gospel account of Christ's death. Hebrews 12:2 reads, "Let us fix our eyes on Jesus, the author and perfecter of our faith, who for the joy set before him endured the cross, scorning its shame, and sat down at the right hand of the throne of God." Jesus didn't enjoy the cross. Instead, He endured the cross for the joy that should follow.

Hannah of the Old Testament is a beautiful example of a woman who found joy despite tough times and difficult choices. Hannah was barren, and her husband's second wife, Peninnah, provoked Hannah to the point of tears about her lack of children. Hannah prayed for a child and promised she would give the child to the Lord if her prayer was answered.

Hannah kept her promise and presented her four-year-old son, Samuel, to be raised by the wicked men at the temple. Then Hannah returned to the conflict in her home and a woman who hated her. Yet, after handing over Samuel and returning home to an unchanged situation, she was able to say, "My heart rejoices in the LORD; in the LORD my horn is lifted high" (1 Samuel 2:1). Her heart was filled with joy.

Hannah was able to sing this psalm with the empowerment of God. Her focus wasn't on her problems, but instead on the Lord, and joy was hers.

Sixty-one

DWELLING IN JOY

KAREN O'CONNOR

H ow can we thank God enough for you in return for all the joy we have in the presence of our God because of you?" (1 Thessalonians 3:9).

When we are faithful to God, through practice and trust, we cannot help but exude joy. This is what Paul saw in the Thessalonians. And the joy he witnessed inspired him to gratitude.

Joy and gratitude are entwined. As we praise and thank God, we are filled with joy, and as we express joy, our hearts again turn to gratitude.

Jesus is our model for a joy-filled life. Joy marked His entry into the world when the angel announced, "Do not be afraid. I bring you good news of great joy that will be for all the people" (Luke 2:10). Then as He prepared to leave the earth, Jesus encouraged His followers to live in His fullness: "I have told you this so that my joy may be in you and that your joy may be complete" (John 15:11). Paul listed joy as one of the fruits of the Spirit (Galatians 5:22), and he reminded the Galatians to bear witness of the

Spirit in their lives: "Since we live by the Spirit, let us keep in step with the Spirit" (Galatians 5:25).

I believe that same reminder applies to us today. We too must keep in step with the Spirit by echoing the words of the psalmist: "My mouth shall praise You with joyful lips" (Psalm 63:5, NKJV). Regardless of what is going on in our lives, we can respond with a heart full of joy because we know that our redeemer lives, that all things work together for good to those who love God, that our Lord will never leave us nor forsake us. Joy is the natural response to such jubilant promises!

Richard Foster writes, "If we fill our lives with simple good things and constantly thank God for them, we will know joy." Fill your life today with "simple good things"—a beautiful sunset, homemade soup, a loved one's voice on the phone, children playing and laughing, a cup of mint tea, a long walk with a good friend, time to read, time to pray.

Gratitude leads to joy and joy to gratitude. And it's contagious! Spread it around—like apple butter on hot muffins. You will create such a fragrant aroma that everyone you come into contact with will want to get closer. What an opportunity this is to share the true source of your joy and gratitude—Jesus Christ—and to invite others into a relationship of their own with Him.

"Enter His gates with thanksgiving and His courts with praise; give thanks to Him and praise His name" (Psalm 100:4).

Sixty-two

A LIFESTYLE OF PRAISE

RUTH MYERS

In the Bible, praise is closely linked with worship and thanksgiving. Through all three we honor and enjoy God. It helps me to think of worship as a beautiful crown adorned with two brilliant jewels. One jewel is praise, the other thanksgiving.

Throughout the Bible people expressed their worship in several ways. They bowed before God, often with a sense of awe, to honor Him and show their devotion. They offered special gifts to Him, the chief gift being themselves.

Today, as in Bible times, worship includes yielding to God as our Lord and Master. We see this in Romans 12:1, where God asks us to offer Him our bodies, our lives, our entire person. This, He says, is true worship.

In genuine spiritual worship, we bow before the Most High God, the most merciful and reliable and winsome of all beings, and we crown Him as Lord of all that we are. We consent to His gracious transforming work in our lives; we agree that He can work in us, so that we'll be willing and able to do His will. In other words, we choose to let Him be God in our lives. This is our greatest privilege, the highest thing we can do.

Worship also includes adoring God, admiring Him, appreciating Him, and letting Him know how grateful we are for His mighty works and the blessings He bestows on us. Thus worship includes praise and thanksgiving. As in ancient times, all three—worship, praise, and thanksgiving—overlap as we glorify and enjoy God. Sometimes we do this in speaking, sometimes in singing, sometimes in silent reverence.

In thanksgiving we express gratitude to the Lord for His love and goodness to us and to others, for His constant acts of care, and for His gifts, including the spiritual blessings He has lavished upon us.

In praise, we admire God for who He is and what He does. Praise can be quiet and meditative. But it can also include celebrating and exulting in the Lord's majesty and splendor, His sovereignty, His limitless power, and His bountiful love—which we do not in the least deserve. In praise we extol our wonderful God; we exalt and magnify Him. Praise includes speaking highly of God to other people, as well as directly to Him.

So mounted in the crown of worship—the basic act of offering God our lives, of honoring Him as God—are the jewels of praise and thanksgiving. Jewels that radiate the glory of God, to His delight and ours.

It's fine if we blend worship, praise, and thanksgiving any way we like. God isn't in the least concerned if we say "Thank You" when "I praise You" or "I worship You" might be more appropriate. And it doesn't matter whether our words are stumbling or eloquent. God looks on the heart; He's searching for people who simply want to honor Him.

A life of praise may appeal to you. But what does it involve? You may be puzzled about what it means to praise continually and give thanks always, in every situation. Won't this lead to denying your true feelings? Does it mean that when you stub your toe or hit your thumb with a hammer, your spontaneous response must be "Thank You, Lord"? Isn't it dishonest to give thanks if you don't feel thankful?

Several things have helped settle these questions for me.

One is that the Bible doesn't command us to feel thankful in every situation. It doesn't command us to manufacture positive feelings. Instead, it commands us to give thanks (1 Thessalonians 5:18). As Dr. John G. Mitchell, co-founder of Multnomah School of the Bible put it, "To give thanks when you don't feel like.it is not hypocrisy; it's obedience."

This does not mean you should deny your negative thoughts and feelings and attitudes, sweeping them under some inner emotional rug. It doesn't mean you should repress them into some deep cavern where, again and again, they can sneak back into your thoughts, press you into unwise choices, and filter past your defenses to pollute the emotional atmosphere around you.

Notice that David and the other psalmists were honest about their feelings, facing them and telling God about them. They knew how to pour out their hearts before Him (Psalm 62:8). Often they praised God first, and then expressed their disturbed emotions, their perplexities, even their complaints. After this they went on to praise God again, despite their struggles. They did not deny their feelings or simply ignore them. Nor did they wallow in them until they'd all but drowned. And it doesn't seem that they postponed their praise until they had worked through their emotions and felt better. Instead, they mingled an honest pouring out of their feelings with sincere, God-honoring praise.

Take, for example, Psalm 42. The psalmist composed this song in a time of exile and oppression, when he felt deeply disturbed and downcast. People were saying, "Where is your God—why doesn't He do something for you if He's the true and living God?" The psalmist told God how troubled his heart was. But even as he did so, he honored God, speaking of Him as "the living God...my God...the God of my life...God my Rock...the help of my countenance" (NKJV). His every reference to God showed his desire to exalt and glorify Him.

What happens when we follow the example of the psalmists—when we express our impressions and feelings yet choose to keep praising in spite of how things seem to us? I find that sooner or later (often sooner) the Lord releases me from being a slave to my distressing emotions. He unties the tight knots within me and settles my feelings, though He may not answer my questions about how He's handling my affairs. And when at times praise does not quickly bring inner freedom and joy, I can say, "Lord, I can't praise You in the same way I did last week (or last year). I can't seem to respond to You with the same sense of delight and celebration. But I do choose to lift You high, praising You for what You are and what You mean to me."

Life—and praise—isn't always a feast of pure, simple gladness. Don't you find that in many situations you can experience both pleasant and unpleasant emotions? Like Paul, you can be "sorrowful yet always rejoicing" (2 Corinthians 6:10, NKJV). You can grow and suffer in this fallen world, yet you can learn to rejoice. You can learn to triumph in your hope, in your tribulations and the good things they produce in your life—and above all, in God Himself (Romans 8:22-23; 5:2-3,11).

Sixty-three

True Worship

ROSALIND RINKER

he Good Shepherd knows what His sheep need. They need the pastures of being together with one another, but they also need the quiet waters of intimate security—security that comes from being alone with Him in the secret places.

"My sheep hear My voice…and they follow Me" (John 10:27, NKJV).

When have you heard His voice and followed Him into His secret place? When have you found rest in just being with Him?

Being human, we tend to be heavy-handed in one direction or the other. Depending on our personality traits, some of us tend either toward always being with people or always being alone. These preferences carry over into our prayer lives. It is just as eccentric to leave all praying until prayer-meeting night as it is to insist that religion is a private matter and do all our praying alone. Actually, it is quite possible to become so ingrown in our relationships with God that we escape to the closet, labeling it "virtue."

None of us should hide behind the alibi that "this is the way I am." None of us should say that, due to our own reservations, we are unable to be at ease in the presence of other believers, or that we are unable to pray with them. By the same token none of us should say that we cannot learn to be alone in a room for an hour or more with God. In time and with willingness anyone can learn to do both. To have one without the other is like having day without night. They complement one another; they help us to become whole persons.

But the Shepherd will not drive you. He will not drive you either to share the joys of praying with others or to the intimacy of praying alone. He will wait. He will draw you and keep drawing you until you begin to respond. He waits for you to begin to speak to Him and to respond from love's freedom, not from love's compulsion. When you are ready, you will find that He has been waiting for you, conscious of you all the time.

Here it might be good to ask yourself, "What does worship really mean to me?" I fail to understand how it is possible to give the Lord full attention, even when we are alone, unless we know something of the real meaning of conscious worship.

True worship takes place within the quietness of the individual. True worship is subjection to Jesus Christ. True worship depends upon the kind of God you worship. True worship is not conditioned by any religious atmosphere. It is like a well of water springing up from within the heart of the lover for the beloved.

It is when I am worshiping God that my heart is cleansed, that I am assured of His great love, which has taken full responsibility for me. It is then that the Cross and the sufferings of Christ awaken my heart to know more and more of the depth of His love. It is when I am worshiping and lost in wonder, and my conscious and unconscious selves pour out love, that I become a whole person.

Sixty-four

THE GIFT OF HIS JOY

CATHERINE MARSHALL

Joy is one of the fruits of the Holy Spirit promised to us. Yet perhaps some of us have misunderstood this word. We may think of joy as the exhilaration of prayers being miraculously answered, of the happiness of life going smoothly because of God's blessing on it, or the emotional euphoria of the singing and rejoicing of God's people in invigorating fellowship.

While God often graciously grants us these blessings, the joy of the Spirit is something deeper. The promise is not that the Christian will have only joyous circumstances, but that the Helper will give us the supernatural gift of joy in whatever circumstances we have. It is Christ's own joy that is pledged to us. Through the Spirit, the risen and glorified Lord will Himself take up residence in our cold hearts, and along with Him comes His joy.

Why have we not understood Jesus' joy? Why has Christendom distorted Scripture by insisting so repeatedly upon the picture of our Lord as "a man of sorrows and acquainted with grief?" (Isaiah 53:3, NKJV).

Of course He was acquainted with grief; He had come to earth in the flesh for the specific purpose of destroying all of Satan's grief-wreckage. Jesus spent His days going about looking into pain-racked eyes and in summary fashion—with delight—releasing men and women from the enemy's bondages. These were joyous tasks because the Lord of life loathed sickness and disease and broken relationships and insanity and death. So day by day, He left behind a string of victories.

And the greatest victory of all lay ahead—the cross. Isaiah, in writing of the Messiah to come as being a "man of sorrows and acquainted with grief," was foretelling the agony of that cross. Yet even there "Jesus...for the joy that was set before Him endured the cross" (Hebrews 12:2, NKJV). So the writer of Hebrews is telling us that Jesus of Nazareth was possessed of more gladness and more joy than all other human beings.

But there is even more. Jesus has promised us not just the extraordinary gladness other men saw in Him while He walked the earth. We, being supremely blessed by living in this era of the Holy Spirit, also are pledged the joy of the victorious, resurrected and glorified Lord. This supernatural joy then, is the joy of the Spirit.

How then, do we get the Spirit's joy? Recognize that it is more likely to come not when things are going well, but whenever we are faced with adversity or problems. This is our opportunity to claim part of our inheritance as a child of the King.

In order to do that, we have to allow Jesus to give us His perspective on our situation. Illness, ill will, accidents, poverty, injustice, broken homes are still with us because in our world there is still much mop-up work left from Satan's wreckage. Once a Christian asks for and receives the gift of the Spirit, he has enlisted in the mop-up crew. Then he will be the target not only for his share of the difficulties that are a part of our humanness, but also those special darts Satan reserves for all Spirit warriors.

Jesus' perspective also includes the long view. Our human view is myopic because it is so self-centered. He insists that we see ourselves as one tiny link in a long line of God's men and women enlisted in the mopping-up process and looking forward not only to a celestial city, but to a time when earth itself will become the kingdom of God ruled by Him, the victorious Christ.

So what is your problem? No matter how bad it is, claim Jesus' own perspective, His own joy in the midst of it. Then really open yourself to that joy and be ready to receive the surprise of your life.

THE PASSIONATE LIFE

LOIS MOWDAY RABEY

G oing a little farther, [Jesus] fell with his face to the ground and prayed, 'My Father, if it is possible, may this cup be taken from me. Yet not as I will, but as you will'" (Matthew 26:39).

Jesus, God the Son, in the Garden of Gethsemane—fell to the ground on His face!

Have you ever been flat on the ground before God? Broken?

If you have not, then the truly passionate life has not been part of your experience, either. Oh, we can experience worldly passion for worldly things. But the passion one experiences when broken before God is not of this world.

When Jesus was on His face in the garden, He gave us our highest example of a life filled with passion. He suffered what we cannot describe with words—willingly—at the hands of His Father—for us.

Are we not moved to the point of revulsion when we think of the connotation of the word "passion" today? One of the meanings of passion is related to sexual desire. But in our society that has become the only meaning. To be a passionate person implies that we are sexually expressive in an intense way. To be less than that, according to the world, is to be something less than whole.

To live with a measure of full joy means to have a passion for Christ. But, as the saying goes, "Mere talk leads only to poverty."

There is no poverty worse than poverty of the soul. Our entire world suffers from poverty of the soul, and that world doesn't even know it. Until we see Jesus on His face before His Father, we do not see our own poverty! To have Someone who is sovereign give Himself to that measure for us—and for us to be less than passionate about that sacrifice—is poverty of the soul.

We have to peer into the garden and then look up from the foot of the Cross in order to understand the Resurrection. We have to get down on our face before God and surrender to His will. We have to embrace the cross to feel His blood spilled for us personally. Only then can we have the fullness of joy over life eternal.

Mere talk is useless. Our thoughts, behavior, and involvements have to line up with a passion for Christ—if we want to have a truly passionate life.

All the passion of the worldly scene is dust compared to one moment in the presence of the Lord, when we know we are fully loved and accepted. This moment may be experienced differently by different people. It may come in a very emotional way or calmly. It may be repeated frequently or just be a moment here, a moment there.

Living in a passionate relationship with God is not definable in words. There is no prescription one can take to achieve the desired result. It is not a once-in-a-lifetime decision to do this or that, to live this list and throw out that one.

It is a journey. It may have begun for you years ago. It may not yet have started. If we are sidetracked in our journey, gazing at the desires of this world, then our passion for Christ will suffer. And our joy in Him will be diminished.

What is important is to begin.

Credits & Acknowledgments

The compiler thanks Janet Guy and Melissa Honeywell for their research contributions to this compilation, and Shirley Honeywell for typing the original excerpts.

WaterBrook Press diligently sought to find the current owner of the copyright for each entry in *One Holy Passion*. Consequently, the company obtained the following reprint permission and credit lines from these authors and publishers:

Kay Arthur, "Facing and Forgetting the Past." *As Silver Refined,* © 1998 Kay Arthur, WaterBrook Press, Colorado Springs, Colorado. Used by permission.

Kay Arthur, "Quiet Time Alone with God." *A Quiet Time Alone with God* by Kay Arthur, © 1986 Kay Arthur, Precept Ministries, Chattanooga, Tennessee. Used by permission.

Jill Briscoe, "The Joy-Filled Christian." Used with permission from *Can a Busy Christian Woman Develop Her Spiritual Life?* by Kay Arthur, Jill Briscoe, and Carole Mayhall. © 1992 Bethany House Publishers. Available from your local Christian bookstore or call 800-328-6109.

Amy Carmichael, "The Fact of His Presence." *Gold by Moonlight* by Amy Carmichael, © 1935 by Dohnavur Fellowship. Used by permission of Christian Literature Crusade, Inc., Fort Washington, PA.

Amy Carmichael, "Sending Telegraph Prayers." *Candles in the Dark* by Amy Carmichael, © 1981 by Dohnavur Fellowship. Used by permission of Christian Literature Crusade, Inc., Fort Washington, PA.

Judith Couchman, "The Beauty of Brokenness." Excerpted from *Designing a Woman's Life,* by Judith Couchman, Multnomah Publishers, Inc. Copyright 1995, by Judy C. Couchman.

Judith Couchman, "Under His Wings." Taken from *Shaping a Woman's Soul* by Judith Couchman. Copyright © Judy C. Couchman. Used by permission of Zondervan Publishing House.

Neva Coyle, "The Power of Confession." Used with permission from *A New Heart…A New Start* by Neva Coyle. © 1992 Bethany House Publishers. Available from your local Christian bookstore or call 800-328-6109.

Helen Crawford, "The God of All Comfort." Originally published in *Discipleship Journal,* © Helen Crawford. Used by permission of the author.

Elisabeth Elliot, "The One Thing Necessary." From *A Path Through Suffering,* © 1990 Elisabeth Elliot Gren. Published by Servant Publications, Box 8617, Ann Arbor, Michigan, 48107. Used with permission.

Elisabeth Elliot, "God Calls Us By Name." *God's Guidance* by Elisabeth Elliot, Fleming H. Revell, a division of Baker Book House, © 1973, 1992, 1997. Used by permission.

Colleen Townsend Evans, "I Can't Make It on My Own, Lord." *A Deeper Joy* by Colleen Townsend Evans, © Colleen Townsend Evans. Used by permission of the author.

Colleen Townsend Evans, "Our Need to Ask." From GIVE US THIS DAY OUR DAILY BREAD by COLLEEN TOWNSEND EVANS. Copyright © 1981 by Colleen Townsend Evans. Used by permission of Doubleday, a division of Bantam Doubleday Dell Publishing Group, Inc.

Debra Evans, "The Grace of Surrender." Taken from *Women of Character* by Debra Evans. Copyright © 1996 by Debra Evans. Used by permission of Zondervan Publishing House.

Jean Fleming, "Why Solitude?" *Finding Focus in a Whirlwind World* by Jean Fleming. © 1998 Jean Fleming. Treasure Publishing, Fort Collins, CO. Used by permission of the author.

Cheryl Forbes, "More Than Meets the Eye." *Catching Sight of God* by Cheryl Forbes. © Cheryl Forbes. Used by permission of the author.

Cheri Fuller, "Praying God's Word." *When Mothers Pray* by Cheri Fuller, Multnomah Publishers, Inc. Copyright 1997, by Cheri Fuller. Used by permission.

Jeannette Clift George, "The Wisdom of Study." *Travel Tips from a Reluctant Traveler* by Jeannette Clift George. © Jeannette Clift George. Used by permission of the author.

Janet Kobobel Grant, "Waiting for God." *Where Is God When I Need Him Most?* by Janet Kobobel Grant. © Janet Kobobel Grant. Used by permission of the author.

Maxine Hancock, "Putting Things in Their Place." *Living on Less and Liking It More* by Maxine Hancock. © Maxine Hancock. Used by permission of the author.

Cynthia Heald, "Fixing Your Eyes on Jesus." Reprinted from *Becoming a Woman of Freedom,* © 1992 by Cynthia Heald. Used by permission of NavPress, Colorado Springs, CO. All rights reserved. For copies call (800) 366-7788.

Normajean Hinders, "The Gift of Contemplation." *Seasons of a Woman's Life* by Normajean Hinders, © 1994 Broadman & Holman Publishers, Nashville, Tennessee. All rights reserved. Used by permission.

Cindy Jacobs, "The Clean-Heart Principle." *Possessing the Gates of the Enemy* by Cindy Jacobs, Fleming H. Revell, a division of Baker Book House, © 1994. Used by permission.

Barbara Johnson, "The Greatest Joy Is His Love." *Splashes of Joy in the Cesspools of Life,* Barbara Johnson, © 1992, Word Publishers, Nashville, Tennessee. All rights reserved.

Jan Johnson, "Enjoying God in Anguished Moments." Reprinted from *Enjoying the Presence of God,* © 1996 by Jan Johnson. Used by permission of NavPress, Colorado Springs, CO. All rights reserved. For copies call (800) 366-7788.

Jan Johnson, "Our Determined and Relentless God." Originally published in *Aglow* magazine, © Jan Johnson. Used by permission of the author.

Lois Walfrid Johnson, "Whatever Darkness I'm In." *Either Way, I Win* by Lois Walfrid Johnson. © Lois Walfrid Johnson. Used by permission of the author.

Gien Karssen, "Peace in Spite of Distress." *Beside Still Waters* by Gien Karssen. © Gien Karssen. Used by permission of the author.

Carol Kent, "Truth in the Inward Parts." Reprinted from *Secret Longings of the Heart,* © 1990 by Carol Kent. Used by permission of NavPress, Colorado Springs, CO. All rights reserved. For copies call (800) 366-7788.

Helen Grace Lescheid, "A Hope Stronger than Our Hurts." Originally published in *Discipleship Journal,* © Helen Grace Lescheid. Used by permission of the author.

Florence Littauer, "Two-Way Communication with God." *Wake Up, Women!* by Florence Littauer. © Florence Littauer. Used by permission of the author.

Anne Graham Lotz, "A Fresh Vision of God." *The Vision of His Glory,* Anne Graham Lotz, © 1996, 1997, Word Publishers, Nashville, Tennessee. All rights reserved.

Gail MacDonald, "Come to the Fire." *High Call, High Privilege,* © 1998 by Gail MacDonald, Hendrickson Publishers, Peabody, Massachusetts. Used by permission.

Karen Burton Mains, "Sacrificing Our Isaacs." *With My Whole Heart* by Karen Burton Mains. © Karen Burton Mains. Used by permission of the author.

Catherine Marshall, "The Gift of His Joy." *The Helper* by Catherine Marshall, Fleming H. Revell, a division of Baker Book House, © 1978. Used by permission.

Catherine Marshall, "The Joy of Obedience." *Something More* by Catherine Marshall, Fleming H. Revell, a division of Baker Book House, © 1974. Used by permission.

Edith Schaeffer, "God's Definition of Faith." *A Way of Seeing* by Edith Schaeffer, Fleming H. Revell, a division of Baker Book House, © 1977. Used by permission.

Edith Schaeffer, "The Meaning of Meditation." *A Way of Seeing* by Edith Schaeffer, Fleming H. Revell, a division of Baker Book House, © 1977. Used by permission.

Elizabeth Sherrill, "Speak, Lord." Used with permission from *Journey Into Rest* by Elizabeth Sherrill. © 1992 Bethany House Publishers. Available from your local Christian bookstore or call 800-328-6109.

Jan Silvious, "When You Don't Know How to Pray." *Fool-Proofing Your Life,* © 1998 by Jan Silvious, WaterBrook Press, Colorado Springs, Colorado. Used by permission.

Elizabeth Skoglund, "Getting Beyond Spiritual Dryness." From BEYOND LONELINESS by ELIZABETH SKOGLUND. Copyright © 1980 by Elizabeth Skoglund. Used by permission of Doubleday, a division of Bantam Doubleday Dell Publishing Group, Inc.

Hannah Whitall Smith, "The Harmony of His Voice." *The Christian's Secret of a Happy Life* by Hannah Whitall Smith. In public domain.

Hannah Whitall Smith, "The Law of Faith." *The Commonsense Teaching of the Bible* by Hannah Whitall Smith. In public domain.

Joni Eareckson Tada, "Seeking God Through Sacrifice." Excerpted from *A Quiet Place in a Crazy World,* © 1993 Joni Eareckson Tada, and reprinted by permission of Multnomah Publishers, Inc.

Corrie ten Boom, "Ingredients for Prayer." *Not Good If Detached* by Corrie ten Boom, Fleming H. Revell, a division of Baker Book House, © 1957. Used by permission.

Martha Thatcher, "Getting God into Focus." *The Freedom of Obedience* by Martha Thatcher. © Martha Thatcher. Used by permission of the author.

Martha Thatcher, "Hearing God in His Word." *The Freedom of Obedience* by Martha Thatcher. © Martha Thatcher. Used by permission of the author.

Becky Tirabassi, "The Blessings and Benefits of Prayer." *Let Prayer Change Your Life* by Becky Tirabassi, © 1992 Becky Tirabassi. Used by permission of Thomas Nelson Publishers.

Anne Wilcox, "Words of Life, Words of Delight." Originally published in *Discipleship Journal,* © Anne Wilcox. Used by permission of the author.

Jeanne Zornes, "The Comfort of Memorizing." *The Power of Encouragement* by Jeanne Zornes. © Jeanne Zornes. Used by permission of the author.

Compiler

JUDITH COUCHMAN is the owner of Judith & Company and works full time as an author and speaker. She is the author/compiler of twenty-two books, including *His Gentle Voice, A Garden's Promise, Designing a Woman's Life,* and the award winners *The Woman Behind the Mirror* and *Shaping a Woman's Soul.* Before starting her own company, she was the founding editor-in-chief of *Clarity,* a national magazine for Christian and spiritually seeking women.

With over twenty years in the publishing industry, Judith has served as director of product development for NavPress periodicals, director of communications for The Navigators, editor of *Sunday Digest,* and managing editor of *Christian Life.* In these capacities she has talked with women around the country, both through formal and informal research, which has given her deep insight and an original perspective on meeting their spiritual needs. She has also worked as a public-relations practitioner, a freelance reporter, and a high-school journalism teacher. In addition, she has earned an M.A. in journalism and a B.S. in education.

Judith has received national awards for her work in religious publishing, corporate communications, and secondary education, and she speaks to women's and professional groups around the country. She lives in Colorado.